QUIT
FOR
GOOD
HOW TO BREAK A BAD HABIT

DR. RALPH C. CINQUE

THIS BOOK IS DEDICATED

WITH AWE AND APPRECIATION

TO DR. HERBERT M. SHELTON

AND

F. MATHIAS ALEXANDER,

ON WHOSE SHOULDERS I STAND.

Dr. Ralph C. Cinque

DR. RALPH C. CINQUE

Dr. Ralph C. Cinque is a graduate of UCLA and Western States Chiropractic College. He did his Hygienic internship with the founder of the modern Hygienic movement, Dr. Herbert M. Shelton, in San Antonio, Texas, in 1976. He later took a sabbatical to Sydney, Australia, to work with the renowned Hygienist, Dr. Alec Burton. In 1979, Dr. Cinque moved to Yorktown, Texas, and founded the Hygeia Health Retreat, which offers a recuperative environment for fasting and Hygienic care.

Dr. Cinque is a founding member, and the current president of the International Association of Professional Natural Hygienists. He is a regular convention speaker for the American Natural Hygiene Society and has written articles for *Dr. Shelton's Hygienic Review, Health Science, Healthful Living, The Journal of Natural Hygiene* and various publications.

The Hygeia Health Retreat is located at 439 East Main, Yorktown, Texas 78164. Phone: (512) 564 - 3670.

TABLE OF CONTENTS

PREFACE

Habit, my friend, is practice long pursued, that at last becomes the man himself.

— Evenus

You can break your bad habits and overcome your addictions. I know, because I have done it, and others, just like you, have done it. All you need is the desire to quit; this book will show you how. It will also reveal how you can build your health more certainly and more easily than you ever dreamed possible. And perhaps most important, it aims to shatter some delusions and falsehoods about health that hold most people captive throughout their lives. Get ready for some challenging ideas!

At various times in my life, I have smoked cigarettes, drunk alcohol, smoked marijuana and drunk copious amounts of coffee. Now, I do not do any of these things. In fact, all of them are completely outside of, and foreign to, my consciousness. I never think about them in a personal way. I don't want them. I don't need them. I am completely free of them.

Since 1979, I have been the director of the Hygeia Health Retreat in Yorktown, Texas. There, I work directly with people to help them change their behavior. People come to the Retreat to break their bad habits. They arrive with one main goal: to stop doing something that they know is hurting them.

Within the friendly confines of the Hygeia Health Retreat, people flourish. They eat fresh, wholesome,

7

natural foods; they exercise; they obtain an abundance of rest and sleep; and they abstain from all things harmful. They grow in health and strength each and every day, as they break the chains that are binding them to their bad habits. But, when they leave the controlled environment of the Retreat and return to the "real world," then their challenge really begins. The stress and pressure of their jobs, their schools, their families, and especially the pressure of social customs can be awesome.

I came to realize that what people need is a method of organizing their real-world struggle to accommodate all of the ups and downs they face in their daily lives. They need to learn how to aim high, even when they are falling short. They need to take control of their behavior without allowing psychological pain or guilt to enter the picture. They need a plan that is simple, effective, straightforward and cost-free. After much trial and error, and many successful applications, the five-step Quit for Good Program was born.

You learn a great deal from people who are struggling against their own vices. You find out what works and what doesn't. I write from the standpoint of my own personal experience, and that includes the emotional stake that I have had in my patients' outcomes. After all, I live on the premises at Hygeia Health Retreat, and when a person stays here for several weeks or longer, he or she is virtually staying in my home. We get to know each other. We often become friends. We relate as people, not just as doctor and patient. I share the joy of their victories, and I never forget that they are always *their* victories, and not mine. I enjoy it when a person establishes an important goal and then achieves it. I love it when people break the bonds that are holding them back and keeping them down. I want people to be free from addiction because I am free, and I know how good it feels. To feel at peace in my mind and at ease in my body each and every day, and to expect to feel that way, both in the near and distant future, is the greatest joy in the world. And it is a wonderful thing to know that these good feelings arise spontaneously from inside of me, and not from anything I have taken. They arise from the total process of living that defines my life - not from any one thing that I do and not from any one thing that I consume.

Getting people free of things they don't need, and shouldn't even want, is what I do. For instance, people come to me as a nutritionist. They often expect me to give them lengthy prescriptions for vitamins and minerals (as if nutrients were remedies). Instead, I teach them how to eat. I prove to them that they can have abundant energy and glorious good health just by eating the right foods. I teach them that whatever role there is for supplements is small. What a relief it is for people to be liberated from the burden and unpleasantness of having to dose themselves with endless pills, powders and potions, day in and day out! Getting people off of wild vitamin crazes and onto first-rate diets is one of the things we do at the Hygeia Health Retreat.

Another example of what I do concerns the ubiquitous backache. Because I am a Chiropractor, people come to me with their backaches and neck aches, seeking relief. They expect me to crack their necks, or pop their backs, or perhaps apply electrical currents to their bodies. They are surprised to discover that I give no importance to any of those things. "But, my back hurts!" they say. "I know," I reply. "But, my back doesn't. Don't you want to find out why? It is not because I have been getting adjustments. (I never do.) It is because I know how to move and use my back correctly." And so, I begin instructing them in how to correctly and efficiently stand, sit, walk, bend, lift, etc. And soon they discover that by inhibiting excess tension and allowing the spine to lengthen in movement, they can stay free of aches and pains without treatment. They rejoice in knowing that they won't be dependent upon chiropractors, acupuncturists or physical therapists any longer! How sweet it is, to be balanced in your own body, without having to depend upon treatment.

Many of those who come to the Retreat do so to lose weight. As you probably know, losing weight can be the easiest thing in the world; the hard part is not gaining it back. I do not offer people pills, powders or liquid diets, because I know that these things, even when they are successful, do nothing to alter the tendency to gain weight. That pathological tendency to convert every spare calorie of food into fat is not corrected by going on "get slim quick" cures. Such programs may work in the short term, but they never work in the long run. Only a complete health-building program, based upon eating whole, natural, high-fiber foods in connection with vigorous physical activity, can reverse the fat-making process in a way that is real and lasting. That is the way we approach obesity at the Hygeia Health Retreat. I care little about the immediate goal of taking off 10 or 20 or however many pounds. What is more important is to start changing the person's metabolism from that of a fat person to that of a thin person. As people lose weight under my guidance, they also begin to lose the tendency to gain weight. They get thin and they stay thin, without diet pills, diet powders or diet drinks. They can be free of obesity for life, and likewise, free of the exploitation directed at the obese.

People also come to the Retreat with high blood pressure and high cholesterol. I put them on a diet and life-style program that corrects their problems in a way that usually supersedes the need for medical treatment. Is it not better to have your health problem resolved, rather than "regulated," "controlled" or "managed" with drugs? There is nothing I cherish more than setting people free from medical dependencies. Dosing people with the alleged "good" drugs, is just as unattractive and undesirable to me as dosing them with the bad ones. To me, the non-pharmacological life is the good life. Getting people drug-free is priority number one at the Hygeia Health Retreat.

You can see then, that getting people *free*, is my life's work. And I don't mind saying, that I love doing it. Life is an ever-expanding quest for freedom and autonomy. And, there is no aspect of freedom more important than health freedom, because every other value in life depends upon it. It is the sheer love of being alive that we experience when we are healthy, that nurtures our capacity to love others. It is the vitality that comes from being healthy that makes exercise a pleasure, learning a welcome challenge, and travel an adventure. The capacity to really have fun in life and enjoy yourself and others depends upon being healthy. Moreover, you cannot cope effectively with life's inevitable snags and obstacles without good health. Good health is the first and most important prerequisite for every other good thing in your life.

It cannot be stated strongly enough that *good health is self-generated*. Treatment of disease is something that you can obtain in numerous ways from others; whereas, health is something that you have to build for yourself. No one else can make you healthy. And there is nothing standing in the way of your good health as much as your own bad habits and addictions.

Practicing a bad habit is like committing suicide on the installment plan. It is an act of self-destruction. An addiction is a bad habit that is controlling and ruining your life. Contrary to what you may have read elsewhere, there is no such thing as "positive addiction." For example, it would be wrong to say that you are addicted to food, just because you need it. You don't suffer just because you desire food. Hunger can be a glorious sensation. It should be a high, not a low. It should be closer to pleasure than to pain. Hunger is what makes food taste good. Hunger is what activates you to go out and seek food. Hunger is what keeps you in touch with your body's fluctuating need for food. I felt sorry for Scarlet O'Hara when she said in *Gone with the Wind*, that, "so help me God, I will never be hungry again". Without hunger, there would be no joy in eating.

11

The need for, and satisfaction of, a normal, biological requirement is never an addiction. There is no morbidity or desperation associated with the pursuit of any true need. Every creature on earth spends its time trying to satisfy its needs. That is what life is all about. In seeking an end, an animal or a person would normally act with poise, balance and control. In such action, the means, or process, would figure just as importantly as the end itself. But, when addiction is present, wild and frantic "end-gaining" becomes the rule, where means are ignored in the desperate pursuit of ends. Such action is never life-supporting, regardless of what the nature of the end involved. Addiction is always a morbid thing, no matter what its object may be.

You can get pleasure from exercise without becoming addicted to it. You can love another human being without becoming addicted to him or her. You can find fulfillment in your work without becoming addicted to it.

Quit for Good will help you to break your individual addictions, and more than that, it will enable you to put a stop to the addictive process itself. Let's face it: if you overcome one addiction, there are always countless more you can latch on to. Your goal should be not only to shed your particular bad habits, but also to break the addictive impulse in your behavior and to interrupt the cycle of dependency that it breeds. That is what **Quit for Good** can do for you.

I have been using and teaching the Quit for Good Program for over eight years. I know it works, because it has worked for me, and it has worked for others, better than any method that has come before. The beauty of it lies in its simplicity and easy application. With Quit for Good, you can be your own therapist and change your own behavior more profoundly than anyone else can change for you.

Read and use this book if you are determined to overcome your addictions and if you are resolved to doing so yourself. **Quit for Good** does not offer you a quick-fix for your addictions, but it does offer you a way to grow out of them. We evolve into our bad habits, and we have to learn how to evolve out of them. This book will show you how.

Let **Quit for Good** be your road map to freedom from bad habits. I promise, that if you follow the program, it will get you free in the shortest possible time. If you have a monkey on your back, such as coffee, cigarettes, alcohol or sugar, **Quit for Good - How to Break a Bad Habit,** will show you how to shrug it off. Get yourself free. There is nothing more important. GET FREE!

CHAPTER 1

YOU NEED A BATTLE PLAN

Man becomes a slave to his constantly repeated acts. What he at first chooses, at last compels... The beginning of a habit is like an invisible thread, but every time we repeat the act, we strengthen the strand, add to it another filament, until it becomes a great cable that binds us irrevocably, thought and act.

— Orison Marden

All of your life you have been told to stop your bad habits, but no one has ever told you how. Everyone seems to know what changes you need to make, but not how you should go about making them. "Just quit!" some people say. It's so easy, they've done it a thousand times. Let's face it: it's tough to break bad habits. It may be the toughest thing you ever attempt to do. And like everything else in your life, if you are going to succeed at it, you must have a well thought-out plan.

Admittedly, there are some people who can just make up their minds to quit a bad habit and actually go through with it. One day they are smoking, and the next day they are not. Simple as that. But, I am assuming that you've already tried that route and that it hasn't worked for you. Dozens of times you've sworn that this would be your last cigarette or your last beer or your last dessert, only to go back to it time and time again. You may have to try something different. If going "cold turkey" doesn't work for you, don't keep banging your head against the wall. You may need to use a different tactic. You may not be able to conquer your addictions by merely ordering them away. But, you can succeed if you follow a serious plan.

We're all used to planning when it comes to positive endeavors. To acquire a new skill, land a better job, create a business or accumulate a large sum of money, we know we have to have a plan. But, since stopping a bad habit is more of a "non- doing" than a doing, we tend to forego the planning. Instead, we rely on will power, hope, desire, encouragement, even luck - but not rational planning. Well, the truth is that problem-solving is problem-solving, whether the problem is technical or personal, whether it is minute or monumental, whether it concerns ourselves alone or a host of others. There is only one way to solve a problem, and that is, with a rational and organized plan.

Imagine that you are an engineer designing a bridge, and you discover a fault in the support system. You know you can't will the fault away, hope that it won't matter, or rely on the faith and confidence of others to diminish it. And you know very well that there is no such thing as luck in the world of physics. So, you have to figure it out and correct it, rationally, systematically and scientifically. There is no other way.

Problems in life are no different from problems in engineering, and they need to be approached in the same manner. We need to have the same no-nonsense attitude toward our lives that most of us have toward our jobs. We need a systematic plan in order to change our behavior - a plan that we can follow just as easily as a blueprint.

The Quit for Good Program does not kid around with your bad habits; it breaks them. Think of Quit for Good as a mechanical system that will take you from Point A (addicted) to Point B (non-addicted) in 5 straight-forward steps. Don't worry about whether it is going to be difficult. Be assured that with this plan, it won't be. Don't worry about whether or not you can do it. Be positive that you can. Just apply each step, one after the next, until you get the job done. This is a plan of action. This is something you can do for yourself. All you have to do is begin.

For the most part, you are on your own when it comes to breaking your bad habits. Society is not really rooting for you. Money is being made off of your bad habits. Lots of money. Tobacco, alcohol, coffee, junk food - these are all billion dollar industries. Who stands to gain anything by your quitting? Nobody - except you. President Reagan declared a War on Drugs, but he could be seen on television toasting his alcoholic drink with other dignitaries. The fact is that alcohol creates more havoc than any other "recreational" drug, and anyone serious about declaring a war on drugs would start by eliminating alcohol. Instead, we get the contradiction that "moderate" alcohol is OK, but that marijuana, in any amount, is wrong. I am not asking for a revival of alcohol Prohibition, and I certainly have no interest in smoking marijuana, but I would expect the President of the United States to refrain from putting any kind of intoxicating substance in his body, especially in public.

It is important to remember that most bad habits, including the legal ones, are drug habits. Alcohol is a drug. Nicotine is a drug. Caffeine is a drug. Theobromine (in chocolate) is a drug. Yet, we live in a society in which there is a double standard when it comes to drugs. If an illicit dealer tries to sell us drugs, we are told to - "Just say 'No'." But, if a respected physician prescribes Valium, or other tranquilizers, we are expected to just say - "Yes." The implication is: drugs are the answer; drugs solve problems; drugs make you feel better. That is the attitude that prevails in Society. When it comes to medically prescribed drugs, it is heresy to even question the need for them or the wisdom of taking them. Turn on the television, and see the endless array of drugs for headaches, constipation, PMS, backaches, insomnia, indigestion, bloating and everything else that ails you. Walk into any drug store and look at all of the pharmacological products that are at your immediate disposal. Take a peek inside the medicine cabinet of practically anyone you know, and see if you can't find over-the-counter and prescription medications galore.

We are a drug-ridden society. We are the most drugged people in history. We poison ourselves, day in and day out, every day of our lives, and we have come to accept this drugging as normal. Whether the drugs are obtained legally or illegally, whether they are considered to be "good" drugs or "bad" drugs, whether we think we have a valid reason or a lame excuse for taking them, the fact is, all drugs are poisonous. It would break a law of nature for a drug not to have poisonous effects. If we, as a Society, would become less enamored with the "good" drugs, we might become more loathing of the bad ones.

The negative effects of drugs are often swept together under the euphemism, "side effects." There is really no such thing as a "side effect." Drugs only have effects. The so-called "side effects" are just as much the regular and direct outcome of taking the drug, as the intended effects. They are just not as attractive. They are only on the side in our minds because we put them there. We think that maybe if we ignore these side effects they will go away, or have less impact, but that does not happen.

We cannot count on Society to save us from ourselves. In fact, Society's message is that it is OK to take drugs, so long as you take the right drugs and get them from the right vendors. The medical profession can't solve our problems, either. Their business is to get people on to drugs, not off of them. Do you think Medicine is going to come up with a cure for drug addiction? Well, try to make a list of all the diseases that Modem Medicine can cure. You'll start to stumble as soon as you get past infections (though there are numerous infections that Medicine admittedly cannot cure, from the common cold to AIDS). To "cure," I presume, is to make people well, to restore them to a state of health, to make them whole again, to return them to a state of normality. By that standard, chemotherapeutic drugs do not cure cancer; cholesterol-lowering drugs do

18

not cure heart disease; and, insulin does not cure diabetes. Modern medical practice, for all of its high-tech wizardry, is mostly a matter of "managing," "controlling" and "regulating" diseases, not curing them. To say that drugs have been overrated as a solution to health problems is the greatest understatement of all time. To say that a medicine is going to be discovered to solve the problems of addiction, is a contradiction in terms.

So, don't think of chemical dependency as being outside the mainstream of Society. There are too many popular poisons that Society sanctions and condones. Alcohol is one of them. Consider that a large quarter of the medical profession actually sanctions the "moderate" use of alcohol. Alcohol is said to "relieve stress." Alcohol allegedly helps people to "relax and unwind." Much attention has been given to a study done by Dr. Klatsky of Kaiser Permanente Hospital in 1980 which showed significantly lower hospital admissions for coronary heart disease among drinkers than among non-drinkers. The implication was that it is better for your heart if you drink a little, than if you do not drink at all. It has been suggested that during those decades of drinking before alcohol causes significant damage to the liver, that it raises the level of high density lipoproteins in the blood (the so-called "good cholesterol") which then protects against coronary heart disease. This is a speculation, but what is known for certain is that alcohol damages the liver (leading to cirrhosis), damages the heart muscle (leading to cardiomyopathy), damages the brain (leading to dementia), elevates blood pressure, increases the risk of stroke, causes testicular atrophy and gives rise to cancer of the mouth, pharynx, larynx, esophagus, pancreas and large bowel (*Alcohol Health - A Report to Congress from the Secretary of Health and Human Services*, January, 1981). It is also well known that even brief drinking sprees in apparently healthy individuals result in premature heart-beats and arrhythmias, including atrial fibrillation. How, under any circumstances, could alcohol be considered "good" for the heart?

There is also a growing concern about birth defects and mental retardation among children born of women who drink during pregnancy. Fetal Alcohol Syndrome has emerged as a distinct clinical entity. Who dares to suggest that "moderate" drinking is actually good for people?

Alcohol is a protoplasmic poison. Alcohol is a teratogen. (It causes developmental defects.) Alcohol is a mutagen and a carcinogen. These pathogenic characteristics of alcohol far out-weigh any temporary effect it may have to raise the level of high density lipoproteins in the blood (as if that were an end in itself that was worth pursuing by any means whatsoever). There are still infant medication formulas that contain alcohol. It is appalling that the medical profession refuses to condemn alcohol outright.

The medical profession should likewise speak out against the evils of coffee-drinking. Few people realize it, but coffee-drinking is extremely harmful. If you won't take my word for it, consider what Bruce Ames, Ph.D., chairman of the Department of Biochemistry at UC Berkeley has to say about it:

"Coffee, which contains a considerable amount of burnt material, including the mutagenic pyrolysis product methylglyoxal, is mutagenic. However, one cup of coffee also contains about 250 mg. of the natural mutagen chlorogenic acid, highly toxic atractylosides, the glutathione transferase inducers kahweal palmitate and cafestol palmitate and about 100 mg. of caffeine, which inhibits a DNA repair system and can increase tumor yield and cause birth defects at high levels in several experimental species. There is preliminary, but not conclusive epidemiologic evidence that heavy coffee drinking is associated with cancer of the ovary, bladder, pancreas and large bowel."

— From an article entitled: "Dietary Carcinogens and Anticarcinogens", *Science*, Vol. 221.

So much for that pleasant morning cup of coffee! Many people drink tea as an alternative, not realizing that it contains as much caffeine as coffee, plus a stiff dose of theophylline, a toxic alkaloid. Caffeine addiction starts early in life with the introduction of chocolate to the diet. It then progresses to "soft drinks," to which caffeine has been artificially added. That special lift that our kids get from drinking Coke and Pepsi is a caffeine-induced drug high. The soft drink bottlers are very clever. They show up at Little League games with free beverages for the kiddies. Get them hooked when they are young, and they will be customers for life. Caffeine is also commonly added to headache remedies, allegedly because it relieves vascular congestion. The irony is that taking caffeine ultimately causes headaches. Adding caffeine to a headache formula serves mostly to get people hooked on the product.

Fortunately, the situation is much better in connection with tobacco, for there is widespread recognition of the evils of smoking. But it is important to note that although the Secretary of Health denounces the tobacco companies for their deceptive advertising, the United States government still grants subsidies to tobacco growers and encourages the sale of American cigarettes all over the world.

Society does not want you to stop your drug habits. It wants you to steer your drug addictions to socially accepted avenues. Be like everybody else. Be a "social drinker." Be a "coffee achiever." If necessary, switch to "light" beer and de-caffeinated coffee, but keep taking the same poisons that everybody else takes. Get your drugs through the right channels, and there won't be a stigma. Take care of yourself, but don't disturb the system. Don't rock the boat. Don't get carried away with self-improvement to the point that you become a crank or nuisance.

Well, I say, don't set any limits on your own personal progress. Don't settle for anything less than a complete abandonment of self-destructiveness, in all its forms. You can't change Society, but neither do you have to fit into Society's mold. You can do better for yourself than Society would have you do.

The Quit for Good Program is a do-it-yourself method to overcome bad habits like coffee and tobacco and alcohol. Quit for Good can also be used very effectively to deal with any kind of junk food habit. However, it is not meant for hard-core drug addictions. Those who are addicted to such drugs as heroin or cocaine should seek professional help and be willing to enter a supervised recovery program. The same is true for serious alcoholics. Anyone who drinks when he drives is a menace to himself and others. Only a so-called "moderate" drinker could successfully stop with Quit for Good. But, it is an important distinction to make that alcohol is legal, whereas drugs, like heroin and cocaine, are not. As it stands now, when you use these drugs, not only do you injure yourself, but you commit a major crime that can get you into serious trouble. You are a criminal in the eyes of the law when you use them. You have to deal with criminals and engage in criminal transactions to obtain them. And, you can kill yourself with one dose. So, if you are using these drugs, don't hesitate to get professional help immediately. Make it the main priority of your life to get off them. Every other value you have depends on it. Put everything else on hold and get the professional help you need. Later on, I will have more to say about what that professional help should entail.

If you are not a serious alcoholic or hard drug user, The Quit for Good Program may be all you need to conquer your bad habits. You can do it yourself if you believe you can. All of the psychological and logistical tools you need are contained in the Five Steps of the Quit For Good Program which are presented in the next chapter.

CHAPTER 2

THE FIVE STEP PROGRAM

"How shall I a habit break?"
As you did that habit make.
As you gathered, you must lose;
As you yielded, now refuse.
Thread by thread, the strands we twist
Til they bind us neck and wrist.
Thread by thread, the patient hand
Must untwine ere free we stand.

— John Boyle O'Reilly

I have never forgotten what my seventh grade teacher used to say, that, "You wake up into a whole new world every morning." Today is brand new. You can live it any way you want to. Today is in sequence with all of the yesterdays that preceded it, but it is not bound by them. Determinism may be a valid theory in history, but it does not reign over individual human behavior. You always have a choice. You don't have to be the same person today that you were yesterday. You can choose your direction and your response every conscious moment of your life. You are not a robot, and you are not a slave. And, you don't have to be a creature of habit.

What is a habit? And why do people develop habits? A habit can be defined as an acquired, semi-automatic behavior, that a person performs repeatedly. Habits refer to the actions that we perform over and over again without much thought, because they give us pleasure, or relief from discomfort, or just because we are used to performing them. But, the hallmark of every habit is not so much its periodicity (the fact that it is repeated), but rather its automaticity (the fact that we do it without thinking). Habits become ingrained in our subconscious minds. When we engage in a habit, we are acting only semi-consciously. In a sense, we are not fully awake when we practice our habits; we are functioning from a low level of awareness.

Awareness refers to our perception of ourselves and our surroundings. We all manifest different levels of awareness as we go about our daily lives. Sometimes we are in sharp focus, such as in giving a presentation at work, or taking an exam at school. Other times, we are awake, but not fully aware. An ominous example is the way some people drive their cars. They tend to do most of their driving in familiar surroundings where the redundancy of the road and the normal course of traffic lull them into a dull, hazy mental state. They selectively channel their attention to the things they think are important, based upon their past experience, such as traffic lights and busy intersections; but it takes something unexpected to snap them out of their trancelike state and bring them to a full, sharp state of awareness.

We fluctuate between high and low states of awareness all day long. But, where habits are concerned, there is characteristically a low level of awareness. Something doesn't become a habit until it becomes ingrained in our subconscious mind so that we can do it without thinking.

Habits can be contrasted with instincts, which refer to the inherent patterns of response that one is born with. Instincts dominate animal behavior. But, humans are reasoning creatures, and therefore, their instincts are less potent and they are easily countermanded. You have undoubtedly heard about "the instinct for self-preservation," but it really doesn't work without thinking. Being hungry, for instance, does not tell you how to obtain food. Either you have to grow food, find food, trap food or buy food. But all of that takes thought and deliberate action.

Thirst is the desire for water, but being thirsty does not tell you where water can be found. If you are lost in the desert and dying of thirst, instinct will not tell you that water is trapped in the stems of the cactus plants. Animals live by instinct, but humans have to think to survive.

However, you were endowed with one instinct at birth that you never outgrow: *the capacity to reject poisons.* Your body rebels against being poisoned, and the more healthy and robust you are, the more vigorously your body does so. But, if a poison is repeatedly given, your body's objections to it become increasingly faint. In the body's adaptation to chronic poisoning, toleration takes place, which is accompanied by a weakening of the rejection response. By the time a bad habit becomes well established, the body's natural repugnance to it may be almost completely silenced. Yet, it is never altogether extinguished, and abstinence is the key to bringing it back to life.

Why do human beings acquire bad habits so easily? After all, we do not see animals in Nature sucking smoke into their lungs or poisoning themselves in other ways for the fun of it. Yet, all over the globe, and throughout history, people have engaged in the most appalling and destructive habits. Consider what happened when the Europeans first came to America. Columbus found the native Americans smoking tobacco, mostly in connection with religious rituals. He brought it back to Europe with him, and by 1556, the first tobacco plantation was begun in France. Within two generations, the entire male population of Western Europe was hooked on tobacco smoking. At the same time, Columbus introduced the Indians to alcohol, and in no time, alcoholism spread across the two continents of the Americas like a wildfire. The white man and the red man came face to face at a crucial juncture in history, and the first thing they did was exchange vices.

All habits are acquired. They are man-made. You cultivate your likes and dislikes, and you learn to like the things you are used to doing. Take food, for example. Asians are not born with a love for rice. It is part of their culture, and by the time they reach school age, they are used to eating it every day. Mexican people cultivate their love for tortillas and beans. The only food you are born liking is your mother's milk. After that, your food preferences are a matter of trial and error and of following the example of others. It is likely that because we are free-thinking, independent creatures, we are more vulnerable to forming bad habits than animals are. Our minds can go in any direction, including directions that violate the needs of our bodies. The mind has no limits, so neither does human behavior. Of course, we cannot do what is physically impossible, but other than that, we are constrained only by the limits of our experience and imagination.

People are not only capable of doing the most bizarre things imaginable - they are capable of *enjoying* the most bizarre things imaginable. Our senses are entirely malleable when it comes to associations of pleasure and pain. They are easily corrupted. Our feelings can become completely unreliable as guides to action. Taste and smell can become jaded. People can get used to just about anything. People can condition themselves to relish the very things that are most destructive to them.

What factors go into forming habits? First and foremost is *repetition*. The more times an activity is repeated, the more deeply it becomes ingrained in the subconscious, and the more inclined we are to do it again. This is known in Neurology as "The Law of Facilitation," which states that, "whenever a certain neurological pathway is repeatedly traversed, it becomes progressively easier for that particular sequence of neuro-synaptic events to be evoked." What it means in plain English, is that the more we repeat a certain behavior, the more likely we are to respond that way in the future. We relentlessly carve neurophysiological channels in our brains, just as the moving water of the Colorado River relentlessly carved the Grand Canyon.

A second factor in the forming of habits is the *approval and encouragement of others*. That is what provides reinforcement. The 13-year old boy who sneaks behind the alley to light up his first cigarette doesn't "enjoy" it, in any reasonable sense of the word. He hacks, he coughs, he spits, he sputters. His body screams in defiance, but he keeps doing it anyway because it's "cool" to smoke, and he wants to impress his peers. He enjoys the image of smoking, not the act itself. People are capable of making themselves do things that they perceive to be unpleasant, distasteful and even painful the first time. Yet, they continue because they like the role it puts them in and all the associations that go along with it. And eventually, they do learn to like that which they first found to be repugnant. Our pleasure-sensing mechanism easily becomes warped.

The third factor that goes into habit formation, and the one that makes breaking a habit so difficult, is *dependency* - which leads to addiction. Fortunately, not every habit becomes an addiction. Take sugar, for example. A lot of people love sweets, but not all of them are sugarholics. A sugarholic is one who has to have sugar, who can't function without it, who feels desperate when deprived of it, and who suffers physical and emotional uneasiness when he or she cannot obtain sugar.

In the case of poison habits, the addict seeks his drug not primarily to obtain pleasure, but mostly to escape from pain and discomfort. A smoker who is truly addicted to cigarettes lights up not so much because cigarettes taste good, but because he wants relief from the nervousness, anxiety and uneasiness he feels between cigarettes. Alcoholics drink not because alcohol tastes good to them, or because it is fun to drink, but because they want relief from the physical discomfort and the psychological pain and depression they feel when they are sober. Heroin addicts shoot up, not in search of pleasure, but to escape the torment of heroin withdrawal.

The reason why poison habits are so hard to break is that taking more of the poison temporarily covers up the effects of prior consumption. This is true of coffee, tobacco, alcohol and drugs. Having a cup of coffee gets rid of a coffee headache. The more of it you take, the more of it you seem to need to maintain the status quo and feel normal. If ever there was a vicious cycle, this is it. But, it is possible to break the vicious cycle, because the body does have a natural aversion to being poisoned, and nothing restores that aversion like abstinence. Every time you abstain from your bad habit, you strengthen your body's physiological resistance to it. You add fuel to the fire of your body's natural defenses. Every time you say, "No" to your bad habit, you break one link in the chain that is binding you. In that defiant act of saying "No," you increasingly break the grip of power that your bad habit has over you.

Observe that the ex-smoker tends to be the most vehement non-smoker. When he first quits smoking, he suffers a tremendous yearning for cigarettes, but gradually he becomes indifferent to them. Eventually, he becomes fiercely intolerant of them. It is the ex-smoker more so than the lifelong non-smoker, who will indignantly get up and leave the restaurant rather than breathe second-hand smoke. The ex-smoker relishes his new-found repugnance to cigarette smoke. He celebrates it. He brings the attention of the whole world to it every chance he gets. Deep inside, he knows that he is more alive now than he was before.

The continued practice of a poison habit blunts the body's nerves and senses until there is little or no discernible resistance to it. But, no matter how weakened or suppressed, the body's natural aversion to a poison is never completely obliterated, so long as life goes on. The physiological integrity of the organism to defend itself can be nurtured, revived and brought back to full expression.

Abstinence is the key to doing that.

The process of quitting is so hard in the beginning. It is very easy to fail, and yet, people hate to fail. Not only do they hate to fail, but they suffer real and intense psychological pain when they do fail. A bird can spend days building a nest, but if a storm comes and knocks it from the tree, the bird does not give up. He automatically starts building a new one, without brooding. A beaver can spend weeks building a dam, but if the dam collapses, the beaver doesn't scream and holler. He gets right back to work building a new one. Destroy an ant hill, and the remaining ants will start tunnelling new holes in the earth with the same vigor as before. A spider can stay up all night spinning an elaborate web to catch insects. But if something disrupts the web and the spider goes tumbling to the ground, he picks himself up and immediately goes back to work. Contrarily, if a man spends months building a house, and it suddenly burns to the ground, he is likely to grieve and suffer for a while. He has to fully experience his loss and deal with it emotionally. Eventually, he will get back to work, but not before going through at least a brief period of exasperation.

It always hurts to have our efforts thwarted. Failing because of our own shortcomings produces the greatest pain of all. If we fail repeatedly, sooner or later, we will just stop trying to succeed. We will give up, because we dread the psychological pain of failure more than the physical effects and other consequences of our bad habits.

So, with Quit for Good, we will not set ourselves up for failure and disappointment by making promises we cannot keep, or by setting standards we cannot meet. We will factor out the possibility of failure from the very beginning. If you wish to quit smoking, don't say that you will never smoke another cigarette again for as long as you live. Instead, apply the first step of the Quit for Good Program.

Step 1: Acknowledge your desire to quit, and cultivate an attitude of avoidance.

There are two aspects to this step. The first part - to acknowledge your desire to quit - involves taking conscious control of the actions that have become automated. Declare war on your bad habit, and let the fighting begin. Say it out loud, mark the day on your calendar, and announce to the world that you have begun the process of quitting. Smoking will never be the same for you. Smoking will never again be business as usual in your life. Never again will you carelessly, mindlessly and casually smoke a cigarette. You are declaring a new attitude toward smoking that commences immediately. What was formerly a friend is now an enemy. You are quitting a bad habit, and you are doing it consciously.

You have to look upon the process of behavioral change as a formal endeavor and a personal project. No longer are you going to wait for positive changes to take place in your life by luck or by accident. Constructive change results from establishing the right intention and then employing the right means to achieve it. But nothing good is going to happen unless you clearly want to make the change. With complete and focused awareness, decide that you are going to overcome your bad habit, and that you are going to employ the Quit for Good method to do so.

The second part of Step 1 - to cultivate an attitude of avoidance - really defines your psychological orientation. Think about the meaning of the word "avoidance." Imagine what it would be like if you were trying to avoid someone, perhaps someone who offended you or rubbed you the wrong way. You would stay away from his residence. You would steer clear of his place of work. You would find a different place to hang out from where he does. You wouldn't call him on the phone, and you wouldn't go where you expected him to be. But, it doesn't mean that you would never encounter that person again. You might run into him at a shopping mall. You might encounter him at a wedding. You might come face to face with him in the library or the supermarket. And if that happened, you would handle it. You would minimize the duration of the encounter and try to avoid any unpleasantness. You would not create a scene, throw a fit, or feel that your life was ruined because you laid eyes on this person or exchanged words with him.

Avoidance works the same way in connection with bad habits. If you are trying to give up eating ice cream, it means that you are going to stay away from it as much as possible. It means that eating ice cream will no longer be a regular part of your life. Eating ice cream will no longer be part of your normal, every-day routine. Ice cream will no longer be on your shopping list. Ice cream parlors will no longer be on your itinerary. You won't promise never to eat it again, but eating ice cream will no longer be "business as usual" in your life.

Avoidance may be a more practical objective than total abstinence in the beginning, because it is more clearly reachable. If you demand perfection of yourself from the start, you are likely to be disappointed. If you tell yourself that you can never do something again, you only have to do it once in order to fail. It would be far better to change your attitude, alter your direction, and re-orient your intentions, without making absolute statements that would hold you to perfection. Don't plant the seeds of failure and discouragement from the start. Give yourself every possible chance to succeed by leaving some play in the rope. That way, you won't hang yourself with it.

The commitment to avoid, rather than to abstain, is not meant to encourage cheating. You are relentlessly trying to avoid your bad habit, twenty-four hours a day. You will not schedule any exceptions. You will not cut down to four cigarettes a day or one six-pack a week. No amount of consumption is really OK. You don't want to make any exceptions at all. But, if exceptions happen because you have weak moments, you are not going to beat yourself up or throw in the towel. You are going to pick yourself up and start over again. You are not going to give up just because you fouled up. You are not going to feel that it is hopeless to continue just because you had a bad day. You are not going to feel helpless and incapacitated when you have had a setback. No longer are you going to lose sight of your goal, just because you sometimes fail to reach it. From now on, you focus on the positives, and not the negatives. You look forward, and not backward. You never quit. There's no reason to quit. You forge ahead, no matter what.

The Quit for Good Program aims for total abstinence, but the success of the program does not hinge on total abstinence. Don't call yourself out on strikes just because you hit a foul ball. Don't lose your direction just because you sometimes stumble. You never have to relinquish your will to stop the bad habit. You can let go of the anxiety about having to be perfect because it's not doing you any good.

On the other hand, it is important to realize that there is nothing stopping you from making a complete and total break from your bad habit right from the beginning with Quit for Good. There is nothing mandatory about the tapering process. The fact that Quit for Good accommodates some backsliding does not mean that it encourages backsliding. By not altogether forbidding access, Quit for Good relieves the anxiety about it. Within the parameters of the program, you can move along at your own pace. But, remember that there is nothing stopping you from discontinuing your bad habit all at once with Quit for Good.

With Step 1, we have established the correct psychological framework. Now we are ready to take decisive, practical action.

Step 2: Rid your home of the offending substance, and all vestiges thereof, and commit yourself to total abstinence at home.

Let's take ice cream as an example. If you are hooked on ice cream and you want to break the habit, don't keep any ice cream in your home. Throw it out, give it away, feed it to the cat, do whatever you have to do to get rid of it (except eating it), and declare your home to be an ice cream-free zone. Do away with any ice cream scoops, special ice cream utensils or serving dishes, special sauces or toppings for ice cream, and any other paraphernalia connected with ice cream. Anything in your home that reminds you of ice cream, get rid of. Make it so that ice cream does not exist within the confines of your home.

How do you get other members of your household to go along with this drastic measure? They may have no interest in giving up ice cream. Aren't you imposing on them by expecting them not to keep ice cream in the house? The answer is - "Yes." But, call a meeting and explain to them that you really want to get off this ice cream kick, and that the only way you can succeed is to not have ice cream around. You're not asking them to stop eating it, only to stop bringing it home. They can have it as often as they like, and wherever they wish, except at home. Tell them that if they will make this sacrifice for you, then you will do something for them. You'll owe them one. The main thing is to convince them of your sincerity and determination. Some of them may even appreciate the opportunity to join you in the effort. But, if not, at least get them rooting for you.

Almost always, there are ways of giving and taking that enable us to obtain what we need from others. To win the cooperation of her family in accepting her ban on refined sugar at home, Barbara introduced them to the joys of eating exotic dates. When Bill asked his wife to join him in not smoking at home, he suggested that they celebrate their smoke-free environment by purchasing the new drapes she wanted. Angela and her husband were accustomed to relaxing in the evening by sharing a glass of wine, but she suggested that they exchange massages instead. Wave a carrot in front of someone. Make them an offer that they can't refuse. Give them something they want, and they will be inclined to give you what you want.

Total abstinence at home is crucial to the success of the Quit for Good Program because home is the battleground of behavior modification. Home is where habits are built and reinforced. It is not only because we spend much of our time at home, but because home is where we *live*. Because we live there, home is where we go into our automatic mode of functioning, where we let our hair down, relax and let our automatic pilot take over. Home is where we do things without much thinking, without much deliberation and from a low level of consciousness. Home is where we set up routines and practice rituals. Our built-in patterns of behavior may or may not start at home, but home is where we nurture them, reinforce them and integrate them into our lives on a permanent basis. So, home is where the struggle commences between you and your bad habits. If you can lick your bad habits at home, you have won the most important and decisive battle. Get control of your behavior at home, and you have gained the upper hand in the struggle.

Your home is your sanctuary. It is meant to be a haven, a place where you can feel safe and secure from the hostile environment of the outside world, with all of its dangers and temptations. Your home is the one place where you can make the world be anything you want it to be. You are the king or queen of your own castle, the master of your own universe, the ruler of your own domain, but in one place, and one place only - your own home. Who rules the world? You do, in your own home. Why not make your home the kind of environment, the kind of world, you want it to be, as you know it should be? You can paint the canvas of your home any color you want. Home is the one place where you create the environment - where the environment does not create you.

If you want to quit eating ice cream, home is where you have to begin. By not eating ice cream at home, by not keeping it at home, you will be communicating to yourself, and to others, that ice cream is no longer part of your everyday life. To whatever extent you do have ice cream again, it will be the exception and not the rule. Your carefree days of eating ice cream are gone forever. You have identified the enemy, and it is ice cream. The battle has commenced. Ice cream is out of the house for good. Never again will it infiltrate the citadels of your fortress.

Don't make any compromises with this aspect of the Quit for Good Program. If you are trying to stop smoking, throw out your cigarettes and ashtrays and even your matches (unless you need them for other purposes). Discard your cigarette holder or pipe, if you use one. Wash your clothes, your sheets, your towels and your drapes. Open the windows, and get the smell of cigarettes out of the house. Make it as though no one had ever smoked a single, solitary cigarette there in your home. Declare your house to be a smoke-free zone. That means that you don't smoke in or around the house. You ask your friends and relatives not to smoke in the house. When servicemen come to work on the appliances, you don't permit them to smoke in the house, either. Don't smoke in the yard. Don't walk down the block to smoke. Don't cross the street to smoke. Commit yourself to not smoking anywhere in, near, around or in close proximity to your home. Period. You are a non-smoker when you are at home. No "ifs," "ands" or "buts."

This condition adds an important aspect of control to the process of behavior modification. Habits become so deeply ingrained within us, that we do them not only compulsively, but impulsively. The slightest whim is all it takes to bring on the urge. It is at home that we are most whimsical. It is at home that we are most indulgent. It is at home that we are most vulnerable. It is at home that we are most inclined to give in to our fancies, our weaknesses, our desires. It is at home that we are quick to surrender. If you are trying to give up eating ice cream, but you keep some in the freezer, you are going to have to struggle with it every time you open the freezer door. You are going to be continually subjected to those sudden urges, those intense cravings, which usually occur when we are least prepared to deal with them, such as when we are tired, bored, stressed or depressed. It is at such times that we are likely to say, "To hell with it!" and have some. An impulse to do wrong can arrive in a flash and overwhelm you in seconds. But, if there is no ice cream in the house, it won't be possible to indulge in the fancy of the moment. Lame excuses, alibis and rationalizations won't make any difference when the freezer is bare of ice cream. Sudden urges won't matter when the ice cream is far, far away. Of course, you could jump into your car, drive down to the supermarket, wait in line, buy some ice cream and start eating it. But, all of that takes time, effort, bother and deliberation, which gives you time to think it over, consider alternatives, and perhaps, talk yourself out of it. The interval of time and space acts as a buffer to prevent you from giving in to the whim to eat ice cream on the spur of the moment. One thing you can count on: with this plan in place, you are never again going to raid the fridge, half asleep, in the middle of the night and eat ice cream. The days of reflexive ice cream eating are over. You are taking conscious control of your own life.

What is the main thing that a residential recovery program does for alcoholics? It denies them access. Whatever else it does, in the way of providing them with education, counseling and supervision, is fine. But, first and foremost, it isolates them from alcohol.

36

So, why not turn your home into your own personal retreat to modify your behavior? Be your own counselor. Be the doctor, as well as the patient. Deny yourself access at home, and you will be doing the most important thing that can be done for you in a recovery program.

* * * * * *

Conscious control is the key. That's what we're in the market for. We're not content any more with programmed responses and automatic behavior. We want to drive the car, not just be taken for a ride. We want to be in charge of ourselves, mind and body.

Poison habits are acts of self-destruction. To smoke cigarettes is to commit suicide on the installment plan. We want to live, not die. So how, in this day and age, can anyone continue to smoke tobacco, when everyone knows that it causes lung cancer and heart disease? Smoking damages the entire body, including the kidneys, the digestive tract and the sexual organs. It accelerates aging, reduces physical capacities, blunts the senses and weakens every vital function.

And yet people continue to smoke. How can they possibly enjoy it, knowing what harm it does them? The answer is: *They don't think about it!* They don't *think* about people lying around in hospital beds sucking smoke through permanent tracheotomies. They don't think about the blackened lungs, indurated organs, clogged arteries or damaged nervous systems caused by smoking. They do know that smoking is bad for them, but that is the only message that they allow to enter their minds. "Smoking is bad for me, but I'm doing it anyway." That is the psychology that underlies their behavior. And let's face it: it's not so hard to live with that kind of thinking. Many things in life are bad. Sneaking into the girls' dormitory back in college was supposed to be bad, but we did it anyway. "Bad" isn't always so bad. It is a weak word that does not communicate much. "Bad" could refer to something that is serious or to something that is trivial. If you only tell yourself that ice cream is bad, you may really be thinking that, "Ice cream is yummy and good, but I'm not supposed to have any." That is no deterrent at all. You need to impress upon your conscious mind all of the cold, hard, facts about the reality of eating ice cream. The best way to do that is with what I call an "Impact Statement."

Step 3: Make an Impact Statement listing all of the ways that taking the offending substance hurts you, and read it or recite it every time you are tempted to indulge.

An Impact Statement is essentially a summary of the case against whatever it is that you are trying to avoid. It is a list that includes every relevant and important effect and consequence of putting the substance into your body. Don't be afraid to make it lengthy, as long as each point is meaningful. The more significant objections you can think of, the better. Here is how an Impact Statement might look in connection with ice cream:

I WILL AVOID EATING ICE CREAM BECAUSE...

1.   It is loaded with saturated animal fat, which can clog my arteries and promote cancer.

2.   It is loaded with cholesterol which can harden in my arteries or elsewhere, causing atherosclerosis, gallstones and liver disease.

3.   It is loaded with refined sugar which can cause diabetes, hypoglycemia and dental decay.

4.   It is extremely high in calories which can lead to obesity.

5.   It is a milk product, and therefore, it has all of the objections and ill-effects of milk. In fact, cream, being the

rich, fatty portion of the milk, may be regarded as the worst part of the milk.

6.   It is a highly chemicalized substance with solvents, stabilizers, emulsifiers, preservatives, artificial flavors and colors, etc. The carton is hardly big enough to list all of the chemicals that go into ice cream.

7.   Ice cream is likely to be contaminated with antibiotics, hormones, drugs, pesticides and radiolytic products. Milk is a reservoir for environmental pollutants, and particularly, it is a trap for radioactive contaminants. After such accidents as Chernobyl or Three Mile Island, milk is the first place they look for evidence of the spread of radioactive iodine and strontium 90. The fat of the milk (the cream) is where these toxic products become snared and concentrated.

8.   Ice cream is a highly processed and refined product, totally devoid of fiber, which can lead to constipation, diverticulosis and hemorrhoids.

Now you have ammunition to use against your desire to eat ice cream. As you begin your campaign to quit eating it, make it a practice to read the Impact Statement every day. Eventually, you can just recite it from memory, but in the beginning, it is advisable to read it. Your special senses, like vision and hearing, are the windows to your brain. Everything that gets into your brain enters through your senses. So, exploit your senses! Use your sensory faculties to instill deep within your conscious and subconscious mind the new conviction. Don't confuse this with subliminal learning. In subliminal learning, you are attempting to impress something directly upon the subconscious mind, bypassing the conscious mind altogether. But *the door to the subconscious is the conscious!* Nearly everything that gets into the subconscious mind, passes through the conscious mind first.

The delusions and irrationalities that we hold within the subconscious mind arise from the contradictions that we allow to pass, uncorrected, through the conscious mind. If you get your conscious thinking straight, you will have no trouble with your subconscious thinking.

There is a continuum between the conscious and the subconscious; they are not separate and distinct entities.

An analogy can be made with a computer document. The conscious mind is represented by the work that is immediately visible on the computer screen. It contains the thoughts that you are holding in full awareness and complete focus. The screen is not big enough to display the entire document, so, much of it is stored in the memory of the computer. It is easy to refer back to stored portions of the document; they can be called up just by hitting a few keys. These stored portions represent the subconscious mind: the thoughts, memories and convictions that are not the immediate focus of your attention, but which nevertheless affect your judgment and attitude. The important point is that all portions of the document stored within the memory of the computer were originally entered on the keyboard and displayed on the monitor. Nothing gets stored in the computer without being displayed on the monitor first. Likewise, nothing gets into the subconscious mind without first going through the conscious mind. That is why the key to altering your subconscious thoughts is to alter your conscious thoughts. The subconscious mind is nothing more than the sum of all of the past slates of the conscious mind. The way to affect the subconscious is through the conscious.

With the Impact Statement, we are attempting to drive the right messages into the subconscious about our bad habits, but through the conscious mind. We want to erase from our minds, forever, the subconscious notions that our habits really aren't that bad, that we won't be among those who suffer the horrible consequences, or that other people get cancer, but not us. We tend to hold a lot of false premises subconsciously, and the Impact Statement forces us to check those premises and face up to the realities they hide.

With the Impact Statement, you are cultivating a new attitude, a new set of values, and a new set of reactions toward your bad habit. It takes time, but you can carve a new groove in your nervous system, a new facilitated circuit, and one of your own conscious choosing. Think of it as positive, self-directed conditioning. This is not brainwashing, but it is "brainwriting." You are consciously reprogramming your mind's computer tapes.

Read the Impact Statement every day until you have it memorized. And, whenever you feel tempted to indulge in your bad habit, read or recite it again. Commit yourself to doing that. Make a pact with yourself that you won't give in to your bad habit without at least reviewing the Impact Statement first. It won't be a waste of time. Often, reviewing the Impact Statement will stop you in your tracks. But when it doesn't, at least you will be establishing the right perception in your mind. A look at the Impact Statement takes the fun out of your bad habit. Think of it as your conscience or your guardian angel. It will not always protect you from yourself, but often it will. It will serve as a constant reminder to "Just say 'No!' " to your bad habit. It will force you to make a crucial pause and consciously reckon with your choices.

The content of the Impact Statement can be both academic and personal. For instance, in his Impact Statement about coffee, Randy wrote that, "Coffee drinking gives me bad breath, and I know that Michelle doesn't like to kiss me when I have been drinking coffee." An Impact Statement can be as personal as a diary. It is a private communication to yourself, from yourself. So don't be afraid to include your deepest, most personal secrets, if they are relevant to your bad habit. You don't have to share your Impact Statement with anyone else, and it is probably better if you don't. Be frank and candid and definite. Really let yourself have it when you compile your Impact Statement.

Another important point is that in reading or reciting the Impact Statement, you must really focus on what you are saying. Give it your complete attention. Read it as if for the first time, no matter how many times you have read it before. Don't read it or recite it mindlessly, the way some people recite the Pledge of Allegiance. Read it with conviction. Think about what you are saying, and picture the consequences in your mind. In trying to kick the greasy fast food habit, Jeff vividly pictured the plaque forming in his arteries as he read about it in his Impact Statement. Really dramatize, in your mind's eye, the evil consequences of your bad habit. Make it come alive, and the Impact Statement will work for you.

Now that you are committed to not indulging in your bad habit at home, let's see if we can make you less vulnerable to it when you are away from home.

Step 4: Make a list of the precipitating factors, or triggers, which prompt you to indulge in your bad habit. Think about how you can rearrange your life so as to avoid activating triggers.

A trigger is a person, place or event that provokes you to repeat a certain behavior. Recall what was said earlier about facilitated circuits within the nervous system. A trigger is like a switch that turns on the entire circuit with one push of a button. It may be one particular stimulus that causes a neurological landslide that fills you with a powerful urge to indulge.

Your resistance to indulging in your bad habit is a fluctuating thing. Sometimes it is strong and other times it is weak. A trigger is something that overwhelms your resistance and takes it right down to zero. In one fell swoop you are ready to submit to your bad habit without a fight. You must pre-empt those circumstances. You must be ready with an alternate plan way ahead of time. You need to be prepared for every foreseeable contingency. For example, Ellen came to realize that entering a certain store triggered her desire for ice cream because she dearly loved the kind they had. In no way could she go near the place without wanting an ice cream fix. She made a conscious decision not to shop there any more for any reason. Just doing that gave her a sense of power and progress that elevated her confidence and control. Karen began to realize that she was impatient whenever she had to stand in line or wait for someone, and that made her want to smoke. She figured out how to reorganize her schedule to ultraminimize her time spent waiting. And, in her purse, she always carried interesting reading material. In her car, she always took audio tapes, and not just music, but also learning tapes. As long as she was doing something with her mind, and not just waiting, she could resist the urge to smoke. Steve came to realize that eating pizza or Mexican food turned on his desire for beer. Yet, he also knew that eating Chinese food (which he enjoyed just as much) occasioned no such desire for alcohol. A trigger not only makes the object of your avoidance available, it also activates your desire for it. It precipitates all of your habitual associations and expectations about it.

To get back to our first example, make a list of the precipitating factors that make you weak and vulnerable to eating ice cream. Your plan may call for you not to drive by Baskin Robbins on your way home, if you know that Flavor #32 has got you mooned. It may call for you to call Aunt Sally and tell her that you are bringing special gourmet fruits to share with her instead of the usual ice cream. When going to the ballgame, it may call for you to take along an ice chest with frozen fruit blends, so that you won't be tempted to buy ice cream. Why not try to make the struggle easier? Why not try to insulate yourself from the circumstances that weaken your resolve? You know yourself better than anyone else. You know when you are likely to be weak, and why. Avoiding triggers is not a form of evasion or cowardice. You are simply trying to steer yourself clear of collisions with ice cream. It is a perfectly logical and rational thing to do. When you deliberately sidestep triggers, you exercise your self-control in a decisive and practical way, and it may even spread to other areas of your life. You will become stronger for having done it, not weaker.

You may have to think about it a while to identify all of your triggers. Moreover, circumstances in your life can change, and the triggers can change with them. Periodically reassess your trigger list and bring it up to date. Keep thinking of new ways to lessen your exposure to your bad habit in order to steer clear of it.

Now you are ready to find out how well you are doing. There is no contest unless you keep score, and so it is with Quit for Good.

Step 5: Keep a score card of your indulgences, including when, where and how much, but allow yourself to feel good about your intervals of good behavior in between.

The first benefit of recording your indulgences is that it enables you to identify new triggers. You may discover a pattern of indulgence of which you were previously unaware. Reviewing the score card is the best way for you to evaluate the success of your adaptations. Without it, you are groping in the dark.

Your purpose is not just to record your sins, however, but to record the intervals of good behavior in between. Let's say you begin the Quit for Good Program to quit drinking beer. You are abstinent for two weeks, and then you give in and have a beer. Sure, you blew it; but you also went two weeks without drinking beer, whereas before you were drinking it every day. Despite having blown it, you still have something to feel good about: you went two whole weeks without drinking! And you also have a new incentive in front of you: to try to break that record. If you went two weeks without drinking, then you know you have it in you to say "NO!" to beer, which means that you can abstain even longer. You've slipped, but you haven't completely lost your footing. You may be down, but you're not out.

Imagine yourself in a basketball free-throw shooting contest. You make eight in a row, and then you miss. Sure, you wish you had made the ninth shot, but eight in a row is nothing to sneer at. And now you're eager to shoot for a longer string. That's how you should feel about overcoming your bad habits. Keep shooting for a longer string. Keep trying to do better. Keep trying to break your record. But, you have to keep score in order to participate.

Many people find that a big wall calendar containing large, empty boxes for each day of the month makes an ideal score card. Don't write on the calendar for any other purpose, so that successive days of abstinence stand out like a string of glistening, white pearls. Really feel good about your intervals of good behavior. See the glass as half-full rather than half-empty. If you were accustomed to indulging in your bad habit every day, and now you are doing it infrequently, you certainly do have something to feel good about. You are making progress. You are on the road to abstinence and recovery. Sure, you are backsliding some of the time, but not in a way that jeopardizes your overall prospects for success. As long as you play by the rules, that is, maintain an attitude of avoidance, practice total abstinence at home, keep and make use of an Impact Statement, try to identify and avoid triggers, and keep a score card of all indulgences, you can feel good about yourself even if you do sometimes slip. As time goes on, you will see the intervals of abstinence lengthen, and it will become easier and easier to resist your bad habit. Every time and every occasion that you say "NO!" to your bad habit, you increasingly break the grip that it has on you.

* * * * * *

The five steps of the Quit for Good Program are designed principally to develop your powers of self-control in an *evolutionary* way. Wanting change can easily blind us because it projects us into the future. We think about where we're going, but not about how we're getting there. Wanting something can lead us to employ methods that work against us in the long run. There is a hierarchy to the values in our lives, and sometimes this creates conflict. But, the way out of the conflict, is to focus on what you have to do correctly right now. The Quit for Good Program enables you to practice abstinence from hour to hour, and even from moment to moment. It enables you to choose abstinence, within the most immediate time frame, and it allows you to feel good about yourself for having done so.

The idea is to gain control over your bad habit, not as a final result, but as an ongoing process.

There is nothing more pivotal to your happiness than for you to feel good about yourself. As long as you feel good about what you are doing, and as long as you meet the standards you set for yourself, then you can be happy, regardless of whether you are rich or poor, lucky or unlucky, famous or unknown. Even when tragedy strikes and happiness becomes temporarily impossible, there is usually something that you can do that will increase your self-respect and enable you to go on. As long as you are at peace with yourself, then you can cope with just about any adversity.

What the Quit for Good Program does is give you a way to feel good about yourself while you are in the process of effecting change. It provides an effective and yet flexible framework in which to operate toward change. All you have to do is play by the rules. You don't have to be perfect. If you stay within the guidelines of **Quit for Good**, you can feel good about yourself despite your occasional indulgences. Then you can stop worrying and actually enjoy the process of overcoming your bad habits.

Here again and all together, for you to use, are the five steps of the Quit for Good Program:

Step 1: Acknowledge your desire to quit, and cultivate an attitude of avoidance.

Step 2: Rid your home of the offending substance, and all vestiges thereof, and commit yourself to total abstinence at home.

Step 3: Make an Impact Statement listing all of the ways that taking the offending substance hurts you, and read it or recite it every time you are tempted to indulge.

Step 4: Make a list of the precipitating factors, or triggers, which prompt you to indulge in your bad habit. Think about how you can rearrange your life so as to avoid activating triggers.

Step 5: Keep a score card of your indulgences, including when, where, how much; but allow yourself to feel good about your intervals of good behavior in between.

CHAPTER 3

A LOOK AT SOME IMPACT STATEMENTS

Habit, my good reader, hath so vast a prevalence over the human mind that there is scarce anything too strange or too strong to be asserted of it.

—Henry Fielding

The following Impact Statements are presented to give you ideas on constructing your own. Of course, you can make whatever use of them you wish, but remember that an Impact Statement is meant to be a personal communication, from yourself, to yourself. You must always personalize your Impact Statements. You must discover what realizations have the most power to stir you emotionally and psychologically to say "NO" to your bad habits. For example, does it bother you that tons of apples, grapes, potatoes, rye, barley and other wholesome foods are wasted in order to make alcoholic beverages in a world where millions are starving? If so, include it in your Impact Statement. If not, omit it. If you are a cigarette smoker, does it bother you that the government takes advantage of you, charging you a huge and oppressive tax on tobacco, figuring that, addict that you are, you'll shell out for it no matter what it costs? If it infuriates you to be burdened to pay more of the national debt than others, include it in your Impact Statement. If it merely makes you shrug your shoulders with indifference, then find other things about smoking that move you more. If you drink "soft drinks," does it bother you that the phosphoric acid that is added to soft drinks corrodes your teeth and destroys the thin layer of enamel that protects your teeth from decay? If you care about your teeth, include that fact in your Impact Statement. If your teeth are already ruined and you have already resigned yourself to wearing dentures, then leave it out. Find the things that arouse your defiance and spur you to decide you are not going to put up with the ill-effects of your bad habits any longer.

It would be excellent for you to do some research in compiling your Impact Statement. A trip to the library or to the book store to gather information, or a call to an informed person to ferret more details, would be an expression of your sincerity and determination. Rather than evade the facts, as you have done with your bad habit in the past, you will now diligently seek them out and add them to your arsenal. Don't settle for the relative complacency that exists all around you. You are engaged in a crucial battle with your bad habit, and no one ever won a battle without clearly knowing why he was fighting it.

With the Quit for Good Program, you need to be driven - not in a desperate way, not in a frantic way, but in a controlled and determined way. And, there is no better way to demonstrate your serious intention than to do some *work*. So, use any of the Impact Statements that follow as a starting point, but not as a finished product. Do your own homework. Make your own Impact Statement. Only you can know how to tailor your Impact Statement to make it powerfully relevant to your own unique circumstances and to your own set of values.

I will avoid drinking coffee because:

1.   Coffee is an addictive drug. Think of it as a legal and milder version of cocaine.

2.   Coffee is a teratogen - it causes developmental defects. Pregnant rats on coffee give birth to malformed babies with defective limbs.

3.   Coffee is a mutagen - it causes breaks in DNA molecules.

4.   Coffee is a carcinogen - it is associated with cancer of the ovary, bladder, pancreas, breast, stomach and large bowel.

5.   Coffee contains caffeine, a toxic alkaloid that irritates the nervous system and causes heart arrhythmias.

6.   Coffee is burnt and bitter. It fouls my breath, yellows my teeth, irritates my stomach and damages my liver.

7.   Coffee is loaded with oxalic acid, which binds calcium and forms stones in my kidneys and elsewhere in my body.

8.   Coffee acidifies my blood, impairs my digestion, disrupts my sleep, gives me headaches and leaves me feeling dull and depressed.

I will avoid smoking tobacco because:

1.   Smoking is a filthy habit. It stains my hands and teeth; it soils my clothes and home; it fouls my breath and my body; it yellows my teeth and it inflames and suppurates my gums. Imagine how disgusting it is for a non-smoker to kiss a smoker.

2.   Smoking is an act of war against my body. It blackens my lungs; it chokes my arteries; it sears my nerves; and it hardens my organs. Every cell in my body becomes morbid when I smoke.

3.   Wanting to smoke is a sick and depraved desire that is biologically perverse. Craving nicotine is no different than craving cocaine.

4.   Smoking blunts my senses and makes me less sensitive to all the real pleasures in life. Smoking prevents me from tasting and enjoying wholesome food.

5.   Tobacco smoke contains acetaldehyde which causes cross-linking of connective tissue which leads to hardening of the arteries, emphysema and fibrosis of the liver.

6.   Tars from tobacco smoke contain polynuclear aromatic hydrocarbons that bind to DNA in my cells causing genetic mutation and ultimately cancer. Smoking is the leading cause of cancer in the world. It causes not only cancers of the mouth, pharynx, esophagus, bronchi and lungs, but also cancers of the stomach, kidneys, liver, urinary bladder and pancreas.

7.   Smoking causes hypoxia, which is oxygen starvation. This results in overly-thick blood, which is more difficult for the heart to circulate. Also, nicotine constricts the blood vessels, putting more strain on the heart.

8.   Smoking chokes off the circulation to my kidneys and scars the delicate membranes that filter my blood.

9.   Smoking destroys sexuality. In men, smoking has an emasculating effect and leads to sperm abnormalities and impotence. In women, smoking leads to breast cancer. There is an increased rate of infant mortality and birth defects among the offspring of smokers.

10.   Smoking fills my body with nicotine, carbon monoxide, nitrogen oxide, arsenic, cyanide, lead and other deadly poisons.

11.   Smoke introduces radioactive substances like thorium, radium and polonium into my body. It has been estimated that ionizing radiation from cigarette smoking (based on a 1 pack per day habit) exposes the smoker annually to 12,500 times the whole body dose received by those exposed to the radiation from Chernobyl.

12.   Smoking causes my blood platelets to clump together and my red blood cells to aggregate in a way that obstructs circulation and leads to pathological blood clots. Smokers have a risk of stroke that is 4 times higher than non-smokers. When a stroke does occur in a smoker, it is likely to be much worse than in a non-smoker because tobacco smoke causes spasms in the "collateral" blood vessels that are trying to feed the deprived tissues.

13.   Smoking slows circulation through my skin, impairing nutrition and causing my skin to wrinkle, thicken and age prematurely.

I will avoid drinking alcohol because:

1. Alcohol is a protoplasmic poison. It poisons my liver, it poisons my blood, it poisons my nerves.

2. Alcohol is an addictive drug that breeds physical and psychological dependency.

3. Alcohol impairs my mind. I cannot think straight when I drink alcohol. With every drink of alcohol I take, I destroy 1,000 brain cells that can never be replaced.

4. After the initial effects wear off, alcohol leaves me feeling dark and depressed. Alcohol signals the brain to shut down its production of mood-enhancing endorphins.

5. Alcohol puts distance between me and those I care about most.

6. Alcohol causes pain — the pain of broken homes, the pain of battered wives and children and the pain of self-hatred.

7. Alcohol brings ruin to careers and accomplishments.

8. Alcohol causes accidents. Twenty-five thousand Americans die every year in traffic accidents that involve alcohol.

9. Alcohol causes disease, including cirrhosis of the liver, degeneration of the brain, hardening of the arteries and cancers of the stomach, liver, pancreas, larynx, pharynx and esophagus. Alcohol occasions the production of toxic mutagenic nitrosamines in the intestines which lead to colon cancer.

10. Alcohol causes waste. Tons of wholesome food, like fruits, tubers and grains (and all of the resources it takes to grow food), are squandered to make alcoholic beverages in a world where people are starving.

11. Alcohol destroys sexuality by deadening the nerves that control erection, by impairing circulation, and by causing hormonal imbalances. In men, demasculination

occurs because alcohol depresses testosterone levels, and it impairs the liver's ability to destroy excess estrogen. Heavy drinking leads to shrinking of the testicles.

12.   Alcohol causes flabbiness in my liver, flabbiness in my heart and flabbiness in and around my muscles.

13.   Alcohol causes my kidneys to swell and leak protein and undergo fatty degeneration.

14.   Alcohol damages the nerve cells in my stomach so that I cannot even feel the inflammation and ulceration being caused until the damage is advanced.

15.   Alcohol hardens my mucous membranes and thickens my tongue, resulting in numbness and lost sense of taste.

16.   Alcohol causes cardiomyopathy (degeneration of the heart muscle), heart failure, distended neck veins, an engorged nose, swollen legs and a bloated abdomen.

17.   Even minor consumption of alcohol during pregnancy can cause drastic defects in fetal development, especially with regard to the brain. A woman who drinks alcohol increases her risk of developing breast cancer by 50%.

18.   Alcohol can cause sudden vasospasms in the delicate and narrow blood vessels of the brain resulting in stroke. The risk of stroke among drinkers is four times that of non-drinkers. If the same thing happens in the coronary arteries of the heart, the result can be a deadly ventricular arrhythmia.

19.   Wines contain naturally occurring sulfites, but more sulfites are added to control the fermentation process, and all are highly toxic. Wines also contain a naturally occurring, cancer-causing compound called urethane. Most wine and liquors sold in the United States contain urethane levels that have been outlawed in Canada.

I will avoid eating meat because:

1.   I do not need to eat meat to be well nourished. Plants are my natural foods, and they are available to me in great abundance.

2.   I have to kill to eat meat, and innocent, sentient creatures have to suffer and die. The fact that I hire others to do my killing for me does not lessen my guilt. To eat meat is to commit murder.

3.   Meat contains numerous waste products, including waste products of the animal and the waste products of bacterial decay. In every piece of meat, there is a small amount of urine that has to be consumed along with the flesh.

4.   Meat contains numerous agricultural, medicinal and industrial contaminants including herbicides, pesticides, fungicides, antibiotics, de-worming agents, growth stimulants and other drugs. I cannot wash my meat. I cannot peel my meat. I cannot inspect my meat to know what it contains.

5.   Meat has been known to contain enough female hormones to make men impotent and to disturb the growth and development of children.

6.   Meat is full of saturated fat and cholesterol, which clog my arteries, burden my liver, obstruct my gall bladder, irritate my colon and increase my risk of heart attack and stroke. Even so-called "lean" meats derive over 59% of their calories from fat.

7.   The excess protein in meat damages my kidneys, demineralizes my bones, acidifies my blood, accelerates my biological clock (causing me to age faster) and stimulates the growth of cancer cells throughout my body.

8.   Meat-eating causes my body to stink, and no amount of cologne or deodorant can cover it up.

9.   Raising meat involves an enormous waste of soil, water, grains, legumes, fuel and money. There is no greater harm to the environment than that which results from the production of meat. There is no greater waste of economic resources than that which accompanies a meat-based diet.

10.   A barbecued steak can contain as much cancer-causing benzopyrene as 600 cigarettes. The total amount of browned and burnt material eaten in a single serving of grilled meat is many times greater than that inhaled all day in severe air pollution.

I will avoid eating salt because:

1.   Salt is a powerful irritant. Put salt into an open wound, and it stings tremendously. The salt water of the ocean irritates my eyes when I swim. The salt that I eat pricks and goads my body from the inside.

2.   Salt overloads my system with sodium. The average salt user consumes 10 times as much sodium as his body needs.

3.   Salt disrupts the delicate hormonal balance that exists between my pituitary gland, my adrenal glands and my kidneys.

4.   Salt causes me to retain water. It causes my eyes to become puffy, my abdomen to bloat and my ankles to swell.

5.   Salt causes high blood pressure which would make me vulnerable to heart disease and stroke.

6.   Salt irritates and hardens my body's delicate membranes, and it perverts my sense of taste.

7.   Salt pickles my body in brine. It makes my blood salty, my tears salty, my sweat salty.

8.   Salt disrupts the perfect balance that exists between sodium and potassium within my body that comes from eating whole, natural foods. I do not add mined potassium to my food, and I have no need to add mined sodium.

9.   Salt has been shown to cause a type of stomach cancer called anaplastic adenocarcinoma.

I will avoid eating sugar because:

1.   Sugar is empty calories. It fails to nourish me, and it robs my body of precious vitamins and minerals that my body needs.

2.   Sugar causes plaque to build up on my teeth, which leads to dental decay and gum disease.

3.   Sugar is fattening not only because it is high in calories, but because it makes me eat more. Once I start eating sugar, I can never get enough.

4.   Sugar plays havoc with my blood sugar. It is absorbed like a sudden intravenous infusion that puts my whole glandular system into a state of alarm. My pancreas, my liver and my adrenals are stressed from eating sugar.

5.   Sugar corrupts my sense of taste, preventing me from savoring the subtle and delicate flavors of natural foods.

6.   Sugar is like an addictive drug. I get "high" from eating sugar that is not unlike a drug "high."

7.   Sugar disturbs the ecological balance within my body. It weakens my immune system and encourages the growth of pathogenic yeast organisms within my body.

8.   Sugar is a poor substitute for the sweet food my body really craves - fresh fruit.

9.   Sugar increases the level of triglycerides (fats) within my bloodstream.

I will avoid drinking milk and eating dairy products because:

1.   Milk is liquid meat. Think of it as the blood of the animal pressed through the mammary glands.

2.   Milk is baby food. Cow's milk is for baby cows. Goat's milk is for baby goats. Breast milk is for baby humans. I am an adult, and I do not need to drink milk.

3.   Milk is excessively rich. Whole milk is rich in fat and cholesterol. Skim milk is rich in protein. Excesses of fat and protein injure my body.

4.   Milk is one of the most allergenic foods known. It contains over 100 different compounds that have been known to cause allergic reactions in people. Skimming actually concentrates the allergens in milk. Allergic reactions from milk range from irritable bowel syndrome to asthma and sinusitis.

5.   Milk is difficult to digest. Many people lack the enzyme lactase to break down milk sugar. Milk causes gas, bloating, cramps and constipation, especially in adults. The main protein in milk, casein, is also difficult to digest, and it is known to be atherogenic. Lactoglobulin, the most allergenic of the milk proteins, is not easily broken down by either heat or the body's enzymes.

6.   Milk sugar (lactose) breaks down to galactose, which is known to cause cataracts.

7.   Milk contains the hormone, prolactin, which is known to stimulate breast cancer.

8.   Milk is a trap for environmental pollutants of all kinds, including radioactive products like Strontium 90 and Iodine 121. Milk concentrates environmental pollutants more than any other food. After nuclear accidents, like Three Mile Island and Chernobyl, milk is the first place they look for spread of the contamination.

9.   World health statistics show that nations that consume the most milk have the highest incidence of degenerative diseases, including multiple sclerosis, arthritis, heart disease, cancer and diabetes.

10.   Milk is anemia food, being grossly deficient in iron.

11.   Cheese contains ten times as much fat as whole milk, and this fat is likely to be peroxidized and loaded with free radicals because of the aging process involved with cheese-making.

CHAPTER 4

QUESTIONS AND ANSWERS

Any act often repeated soon forms a habit; and habit allowed, steadily gains in strength. At first it may be but as a spider's web, easily broken through, but if not resisted, it soon binds us with chains of steel.

—Tryon Edwards.

" Should I concentrate on just one bad habit at a time, or should I apply the Quit for Good Program to all of my bad habits at once? "

There is no reason why you should not attack all of your bad habits at once. In the long run, it will be easier and more certain to achieve results. Bad habits are like wolves; they travel in packs. Attacking all of them at once is the best way to short circuit the self-destructive tendency in your behavior.

You should make separate Impact Statements and trigger lists for each bad habit, but you can keep one score card. You will find that your efforts to overcome one bad habit will strengthen your resolve to overcome others. Just don't get picayune about it. Use the Quit for Good Program for things that really matter.

" For which bad habits would the Quit for Good Program not be appropriate? "

As already stated, the Quit for Good Program would not be suitable for illegal, hard-core drug addictions, such as heroin or cocaine, nor would it be appropriate for a serious alcohol addiction. If you are a so-called "moderate" drinker, you can use the Quit for Good Program to stop. But, if you are seriously alcoholic, or if you drink when you drive, then you should get professional help.

" How do I know if I am making adequate progress? How do I know if Quit for Good is working for me? "

Keep an eye on your score card. If the number of indulgences is declining and the intervals of abstinence are lengthening, you can feel confident that you are on the right track. You need to make steady progress, but not necessarily fast progress. Don't set any deadlines for yourself to reach total abstinence. That will only give you added pressure that you don't need.

" If I cannot use the Quit for Good Program to overcome a severe drug or alcohol addiction, what do you recommend? "

I recommend that you enter a rehabilitation center, and preferably one that not only provides control and supervision in a protective and supportive environment, but also provides a total health-building regimen. All of the elements of health must be provided, including fresh air, whole, natural foods, pure water, physical activity, adequate sunlight, and plenty of rest and sleep and peace and quiet.

The process of recovery from drug or alcohol addiction does not depend essentially upon medical intervention. Special treatment may be needed in an emergency, such as dehydration with blood mineral disturbance, but that is the exception and not the rule. Fundamentally, there is no need to give addicts and alcoholics drugs of any kind, and to do so is counterproductive. Drugs are what got them into trouble in the first place. Furthermore, the recovery process is not fostered by substituting lesser evils for greater ones. At the Hygeia Health Retreat, we do not allow people to overcome one bad habit by reinforcing another. We do not deny people alcohol, yet offer them coffee. We do not forbid smoking, but allow people to chew gum laced with nicotine. We do not take away their drugs, but fill them up with greasy meats and refined sugar. Frankly, we make no significant compromises. We prohibit people from harming themselves in any way. We want to alter the addictive process at the physical, psychological and cellular levels. Our job is not only to help people overcome their addictions, but to help them cultivate a new and better way of life. We attempt to surround them with only healthful influences. We try to set an example of life-supporting behavior that they can emulate and take home.

We must never take a piecemeal approach to a behavioral problem like drug or alcohol addiction. Such an addiction does not exist as an isolated problem, but rather as an overall failure of adaptation. Only the broadest possible approach, incorporating every aspect of healthful living, can bring about the total rehabilitation of the individual.

❝ Do you offer counselling and group therapy at the Hygeia Health Retreat? ❞

We talk, we listen and we frequently hold group meetings to enable people to build friendships and exchange ideas, but we do not offer any kind of psychological therapy. We do not fundamentally accept the illness model in connection with the use of alcohol and drugs, although we are the first to admit that disease evolves from the use of these substances. We do not try to analyze each individual's mind to figure out why he or she drinks alcohol or takes drugs. We know very well that people do these things because these substances are readily available, because they give people an unwholesome kind of pleasure, because they provide temporary relief from unhappiness and anxiety, and because these substances are physically and psychologically addictive.

We do not encourage people to dwell on past events in their lives or on their past mistakes. We would rather see them search for their strengths than lament their weaknesses. In the end, we are more interested in action than in talk. "What action does a person need to take right now in order to get his or her life back on track?" That is a question that we frequently explore with our guests, but only from a practical, common sense point of view. We do not pretend to be "mind experts," and we have no wish to treat people like psychiatric patients. We encourage people to take responsibility for their own health by learning all they can about it. We choose to be optimistic, and we encourage our guests to do likewise. And, last but not least, self-bashing is absolutely forbidden at the Hygeia Health Retreat.

❝ Are there any other measures used to overcome addiction at the Hygeia Health Retreat? ❞

Yes, we frequently make use of fasting. Abstinence from food sharpens sensory acuity, as it strengthens a person's natural aversion to poisons. People are more open to making changes after fasting, particularly in connection with what they eat, drink and otherwise consume. After a week of fasting, cigarettes do not taste good any more, even to an inveterate smoker. Alcohol loses its appeal just as quickly.

Fasting promotes detoxification, and it facilitates the return to biological normality. It is amazing, for instance, how quickly the lungs of a smoker will clear during a fast. It is equally impressive to see how quickly swelling disappears in an alcoholic when fasting is employed. Alcoholics, unlike most people, tend to sleep a great deal when they fast. Their battered nervous systems take a complete rest. But, that makes it easier for them to fast, and they always emerge from this state of pseudo-hibernation in a greatly improved condition. Fasting greatly eases the withdrawal from other drugs as well, including heroin and cocaine. Rather than doping these ill-fated people with Valium, Librium or other sedatives, it is a far better practice to employ fasting.

Fasting is less difficult than most people realize. Hunger tends to disappear after a day or two, and fasters tend to feel quite calm and relaxed. The main precaution is not to rise and move about too quickly after one has been sitting or lying down, so as to avoid becoming dizzy and light-headed. Because the blood pressure tends to drop while fasting, it takes longer for circulatory adjustments to take place in response to postural changes.

As long as restful conditions and experienced supervision are provided, fasting is perfectly safe. Contrary to what some fasting books advocate, it is not necessary to administer colonic irrigations, herbs, laxatives or other "holistic" paraphernalia while fasting. For the best advice about fasting, one should consult with a member of the **International Association of Professional Natural Hygienists**, which is a group of medical doctors, osteopaths and chiropractors who specialize in fasting supervision. For a list of such members, you may write the IAPNH at 204 Stambaugh Building, Youngstown, OH 44503.

Fasting is the ultimate form of abstinence, and therefore, it encourages the resurgence of normal instinctual responses, including the rejection response to poisons. The period of fasting can be a time for reflection, and it may augur a new beginning in a person's life.

Fasting is not a panacea, but it is an effective way to catalyze personal change. Everyone should at least be aware of it as an option. For information about fasting I recommend any of the books by Dr. Herbert M. Shelton, particularly, *The Science and Fine Art of Fasting, Fasting Can Save Your Life*, and *Fasting for the Renewal of Life*.

All books presently in print by Dr. Shelton are available from the American Natural Hygiene Society, P.O. Box 30630, Tampa, FL. 33630. (813) 855-6607

CHAPTER 5

WHAT ABOUT THE ANONYMOUS PROGRAMS?

Our repeated failures to fully act as we would wish must not discourage us. It is the sincere intention that is the essential thing, and this will, in time, release us from the bondage of habits which at present seem almost insuperable.

—Thomas Troward

Overcoming a bad habit is a personal project. It does not happen overnight. Few people can do it by declaration alone. Most of us require a plan — an orderly, systematic, step-by-step plan. It has to be something that you can follow just as surely as a road map. But, the road to behavioral control is often bumpy and tortuous, so the plan has to be flexible and accommodating, but still true to its course.

The Quit for Good Program is not the only step-by-step plan that you can follow. The highly acclaimed 12 Step Program of Alcoholics Anonymous has been around since 1935, and it has earned the respect of schools, churches, corporations and governments. It is also strongly favored by the medical establishment. There is no question that Alcoholics Anonymous has enabled millions of people to achieve and maintain sobriety in their struggles against alcohol and drugs. Through its sister organizations, it has enabled millions more to conquer compulsive over-eating, gambling and other forms of addictive behavior. There is only one reason why I would put forward a step-by-step program as an alternative to Alcoholics Anonymous, and that is, that AA does not *work for everyone*. It has its successes, but it also has its failures. It is right for some people, but it is not right for others. I do not dispute any of the claims made for AA. In fact, I applaud their successes and I wish them millions more. Nor do I wish to disturb those who are happy with the progress they are making through AA. I salute their continuous sobriety, because I know how hard they work to achieve it. And to those who have contributed their time and money to AA in order to help others, I have nothing but respect and admiration.

But why should AA be the only game in town? Why should everyone with an alcohol or drug problem or eating disorder be steered into the Anonymous Programs? Why assume that the Anonymous approach is the best approach for everyone? The Anonymous program begins from a certain philosophical platform. Why assume that everyone is standing on that platform? Quit for Good is offered as an alternative to the Anonymous program for those who do not feel comfortable with it.

The Anonymous programs start with the premise that the addict is powerless to stop. He cannot do it himself. On his own, he is helpless. Granted, it is sometimes true. But it is not always true, and a lot of people just don't want to think that way, and they don't want to function from that premise. They want to believe that they can conquer their addictions themselves. On their own power, they want to struggle against their addictions and win.

Tell a man that he is powerless, and it is like telling him that he is impotent, that he is unfit to live. But give him a task to do in which he can express his competence, and you give him the means to regain that sense of efficacy that is also the source of his self-worth.

But one thing a person should never do is transfer his addictive tendencies from one vice, like alcohol, to another, like tobacco. And that is exactly what happens at

Anonymous meetings. People sit around a circle lamenting the evils of alcohol, while chain-smoking cigarettes and pouring down coffee. Tobacco, in particular, is just as addictive and destructive as alcohol. It may not be a lesser evil. In my opinion, all Anonymous meetings should be smoke-free and caffeine-free. Bad habits are like birds; they flock together. It's not good enough to switch from one vice to another. Your goal is to discontinue compulsive, addictive and destructive behavior. Period. There is no merit in doubling up on one bad habit in order to overcome another.

With Quit for Good, we tackle all of our bad habits at once. We don't tear ourselves down; we build ourselves up. We don't say, "I can't." We say, "I CAN!" We let ourselves feel good about every positive change we make, even if it falls short of perfection. We set goals that we know we can reach, but we set no deadlines. We aim for steady, unrelenting progress, no matter how slow. We don't substitute one bad habit for another. We seek to expand our practice of life-affirming behavior and not limit it to just one thing. We set in motion a beneficent cycle, and once started, we never let it stop.

CHAPTER 6

A HEALTH PROGRAM YOU CAN LIVE WITH

Habit is either the best of servants or the worst of masters.

— Nathaniel Emmons

The five steps of the Quit for Good Program have been presented in full. You now have all the tools you need to conquer your bad habits. But, at the same time, you should try to build good habits. A healthful life-style sets a tone of constructiveness, rather than destructiveness, in your life. Healthful living strengthens your body's inborn capacity to reject poisons. So, do more than just break your bad habits: develop good ones.

The science of health is called *Hygiene.* Hygiene deals with more than just cleanliness and the care of the teeth. It involves every part of the body and every aspect of living. *Dorland's Medical Dictionary* defines hygiene as "the science of health and its preservation." More precisely, Hygiene is the branch of Biology that seeks to identify the materials and conditions of health, and how best to apply them under various circumstances in life. The elements of Hygiene are food, air, water, light, temperature, activity, rest and psychology. It is the interaction between you and your personal environment that is the province of Hygiene.

There are certain fundamental truths about life and health that Hygienists refer to as natural laws. Unlike man-made laws, which define how things *should be*, natural laws define how things *are*. The term actually refers to the orderliness and regularity that is characteristic of all natural phenomena. A thing is what it is; it has certain capacities and certain limitations that define its identity and its relationship with other things. For example, in relation to the human body, a poison is a poison. It does not matter if you take a lot of it or just a little; it is still a poison. It does not matter if you take it orally, rectally, intravenously, subdermally or any other way; it is still a poison. It does not matter if you take it in a state of health or in a state of disease; it is still a poison. It does not matter if you take it accidentally or on purpose. It does not matter if your intention in taking it is to save your life or end your life. It is always poison. The relationship does not change.

Hygienists hold that everything in the environment has a certain, distinct relationship with the human body, as being either usable or non-usable, life-supporting or life-threatening, friendly or hostile. We maintain that only those materials and influences that have a normal relationship to human functioning should be taken. Observe that a thing has to be more than just *natural* to qualify as a Hygienic influence; its use must be a normal and essential part of life. Rather than look for foreign and unusual substances with which to stimulate and provoke the body, the Hygienist seeks to gently support the body's actions by judiciously supplying the true essentials of life, removing all forms of interference, and then getting out of life's way. *Biological normality* is the standard by which Hygienists judge just about everything.

"Does the body need it and can the body use it?" These are the most important questions the Hygienist has to ask.

Hygienists recognize that life depends upon a constant process of internally-generated action. Every living organism generates its own energy and acts on its own behalf in self-construction, self-repair and self-defense. In other words, vitality comes from within, and not from without. A substance can only be beneficial if the body is

74

capable of using it. Usability is the true measure of value in the biological realm. And it follows from that, that the means by which health is restored are essentially the same as those by which health is preserved and maintained. Becoming sick does not change any of the fundamental needs of life. Becoming sick does not suddenly enable the body to make use of a substance that it does not need and cannot use in a state of health. Rather than search for remedies, the professional Hygienist deals only with the necessities of life because that is all that the body is capable of using, whether one is well or sick.

Since life, including all aspects of healing, is a spontaneous, biological process, it can be nurtured only by providing the right materials, establishing the right conditions and otherwise leaving it alone. We have to learn to allow biological improvements to take place, rather than always trying to force them.

Hygiene teaches that it is how you live your life, and how you go about fulfilling your biological and personal needs, that determine the state of your health. Health is natural and normal, and it is the birthright of virtually everyone. But, more than anything else, it is the result of what you do. Hygienic measures, such as eating whole, natural foods, staying physically active, securing plenty of rest and sleep, and establishing clean and safe surroundings, are the true elixirs of health. Therapeutic measures, on the other hand, (whether medical or non-medical) treat the symptoms, but rarely do they address the causes of health problems. Hygienists focus on the ways of life of the individual, both to maintain and to restore health. Too often we rush into treatment to deal with our health problems, without considering the ways in which we can foster recovery by altering our behavior. And it is most important that we keep a balanced perspective and avoid giving one aspect of health too much focus. For example, the current enthusiasm for reducing the amount of fat and cholesterol in the diet is a good thing, but it is one-sided. It should not be the sole focus of a health program, for there is more to healthful living than avoiding cholesterol and fat. Hygiene takes a balanced view and equitably addresses all of the factors that pertain to health.

With so many books available on diet, exercise and health, why should you listen to what a Hygienist has to say about it? There are two reasons. The first is that Hygiene is based upon sound, biological principles, not upon the latest fad or fancy. Diet and weight loss schemes come and go like the fashions in women's clothing. Most health writers promote whatever theories and practices are already in vogue. But, your goal is to develop good, lifelong health practices, not to support a popular fad. I find it amusing that so many authors today write about "free radicals" and antioxidants when these terms were practically unknown in the popular press until recently. Everyone is jumping on the bandwagon. However, I suspect that not more than a handful have a thorough understanding of what they are talking about. Today, it would seem that you need a Ph.D. in Biochemistry in order to decide what to eat. But, remember that it is not technical jargon that gives something practical value, and keep reminding yourself that popularity is not the measure of truth. Professional Hygienists devote their attention to the practical and enduring aspects of health-building, without any hype.

The second reason you can trust a Hygienist is that he has nothing to sell you. There are no special products, no trendy nutrients and no exalted remedies in the practice of Hygiene. In fact, we shun these things, not only because they fail to deliver the promises made for them. but because they threaten our most cherished quality of life, namely, *health freedom.*

Health freedom means being healthy by virtue of your own actions, your own choices, and the application of your own knowledge. It means not relying on anyone else to get you well or keep you well (except in an emergency). It means relying upon the normal and abundant materials of life on Earth to sustain you and not upon exotic or adventitious substances. It means being able to travel almost anywhere and know that your needs can be easily met. It means being free of therapeutic dependencies of all kinds.

Here in the United States, we have more medical doctors than any country on earth, yet we have more chronic disease than most Third World nations. We have an army of chiropractors adjusting our spines in every way imaginable, yet our backs still hurt.

Whatever good there is in all of our modern therapeutics, it certainly has not solved our health problems. Let it be known that health is a personal responsibility and a personal achievement. You must live your way to health. There is no other way. Hygiene can show you how.

* * * * * *

When it comes to diet, there are essentially two kinds of people. First, there are those who never think about what they eat and the effect that different foods have upon their health. They just eat whatever is handy and whatever they feel like. Then, there are those who become "experts" on the subject, who latch on to every new theory and follow every new pundit and enjoy tinkering with themselves nutritionally. You are not limited to those two choices. You can be smart about eating without becoming bogged down by it. You can achieve superior nutrition without spending a small fortune on food and nutrients. And assuming that you are reasonably healthy to begin with, you should be able to spend much less money on doctors of all kinds. There are a million and one so-called "health programs", but Hygiene is your only ticket to health freedom.

A Hygienic diet revolves around fresh fruits and vegetables. These are, undoubtedly, the best foods that you can eat. Not only do they provide an abundance of vitamins and minerals and carbohydrates, but they also provide small, but significant, amounts of high quality protein. Fruits and vegetables provide all of the fiber your body needs. They provide most of the water you need. Yet, they are low in calories, fats and sodium. They are highly alkalinizing, which means that they can buffer acids that form in your system. Fresh fruits and vegetables are the one class of food that you can eat to your heart's - and your stomach's - content. So don't be afraid to make a meal out of fruits, especially in the morning. Don't be afraid to forage on crisp, green salads. These foods are really good for you.

The rest of your diet can be chosen from a variety of whole, natural foods, such as potatoes, yams, whole grains (such as brown rice), nuts (particularly almonds), and legumes (such as split peas and lentils). Don't rely on extracts, concentrates or fragments. Fractionated foods may look great on paper, but they pale in comparison with whole natural foods when it comes to actual nutritional benefits. Eat liberally of fresh, raw foods, and what vegetables you do cook, you should cook conservatively. Steaming and waterless cooking are best, but baking is also acceptable. Stay away from fried foods completely.

Avoid sugars and sweeteners, including honey. Don't let anyone convince you that honey is a "health food." It is nothing of the kind. It is mostly sugar and water and bee debris. Fresh fruit provides all of the sugar that your body needs.

Avoid liquid oils of all kinds. Don't be concerned with the debate over which oil is best. They are all bad, and the only question is, "Which one is the worst?" It is practically impossible to extract oil from a food without bringing about considerable oxidation and rancidity. Even with expeller pressing, temperatures of more than 90 degrees Celsius are generated, which is more than enough to begin fatty acid deterioration. Yet these oils are commonly sold as "cold-pressed." It is actually very difficult to extract oil from a food without doing harm to the fat. The oil would have to be extracted at a temperature of less than 45 degrees Celsius, in an oxygen-free environment, and in complete darkness. It would have to be stored in an opaque container, under refrigeration, and used up rapidly. You can see that the making of liquid oil from whole food is a losing proposition. You are not going to protect your heart by putting extra grease in your body, no matter how it was derived. All of the essential fatty acids can be obtained by eating whole, natural foods. Although fruits and vegetables contain less than 1% fat by weight, the fat they do contain is of very high quality, and it more than satisfies the body's need for essential fatty acids. Adding extracted oil to the diet is just as unnecessary and undesirable as adding refined sugar. In fact, it would be wise to limit your consumption of oil-rich natural foods (like nuts and avocados) to small amounts. These foods are wholesome and nutritious, but they contain concentrated fat, and they should, therefore, be eaten sparingly.

The debate over butter and margarine is turning into a comic brawl. The margarine makers point to the cholesterol and saturated fat in butter. The butter boys point to the hydrogenated fat in margarine (which has been shown to cause cancer in animals). I say they are both right. Butter and margarine are both worthless fats that people don't need and are better off without. Try mixing some Picante sauce with your potatoes or rice for a taste treat that far exceeds butter or margarine.

I don't claim that you have to be a strict vegetarian in order to be healthy, but you would be wise to at least aim towards vegetarianism and minimize as much as possible your consumption of all animal foods, including meat, poultry, fish, eggs and milk. Realize that in the long run, the less animal food you eat, the better off you are. A 100% vegan diet is the ideal.

Contrary to what we have been taught all of our lives, there is nothing essential about eating animal foods (with the exception of mother's milk at birth). All of the nutrients that your body needs can be readily obtained from plants, with the possible exception of Vitamin B-12 (which will be discussed shortly). Once you reach adulthood, your body's need for protein is very small, and there is really no advantage to eating animal foods. On the contrary, there are numerous disadvantages. Animal foods, in general, and meats in particular, are high in fat and cholesterol; they are excessively high in protein; they are completely lacking in fiber; and they are likely to contain numerous waste products and contaminants from the animal and from the environment. But what may be more important to us, in the context of this book, is that meat-eating tends to be addictive.

People develop an attitude of dependency on meat that is unlike their attitude toward any other food. They think they can't function without it. They expect to become weak if they don't get it. In contrast, I love bananas, and I eat them almost daily, but I don't suffer if I go without them. There are plenty of other wholesome foods that I can eat. But take away meat from some people, and it is like denying them water. It is not good to be that strongly attached to any food. No doubt, some of this dependency is psychological, but there may be a chemical component to it, as well. The protein and other nitrogenous compounds in meat are stimulants that are capable of arousing people, physically and psychologically. There may be a chemical "high" connected with meat-eating that is similar to the "high" people get from other stimulants. Certainly, a person with an addictive personality, who is trying to overcome bad habits, should avoid meat-eating. It is no mere coincidence that the occurrence of smoking is much higher among meat-eaters than among vegetarians. The same is true for alcohol and other drugs. Vegetarians seem to develop a natural disdain for these harmful things without even trying. Vegetarianism, in and of itself, promotes temperance and sobriety.

It is not true that you have to eat dairy products in order to obtain enough calcium. Almonds, collards, broccoli, bok choy and kale contain an abundance of calcium, and there is a moderate amount of the mineral in all fruits and vegetables. Excess dietary protein and a lack of exercise have more to do with osteoporosis than a lack of dietary calcium. High protein diets virtually wash the calcium out of the blood and into the urine. A diet of fruits, vegetables, nuts and starches can provide in excess of 800 mg. of calcium per day, which should be more than enough for anyone. The body's actual need is much less - on the order of 400 mg. per day. People seem to need more calcium because of their high protein intake, their prodigious consumption of coffee (which contains much calcium-binding oxalic acid) and their enormous consumption of refined carbohydrates, particularly white sugar (which has a demineralizing effect upon bones). Special mention should be made of "soft drinks," which are laced with calcium-depleting phosphoric acid. Stop the intake of these calcium-robbers, and the amount of calcium in ordinary fruits and vegetables will more than suffice. In the words of John McDougall, M.D., author of *The McDougall Plan*, "Milk is just liquid meat." All of the objections that can be raised against meat-eating also apply to milk. Man is the only creature in Nature who drinks milk beyond infancy and who takes milk from other species. But there are millions of people in the world (many of them Asians) who live their entire lives without consuming milk, and yet they remain healthy and well-nourished. They do not suffer from a lack of milk. It is the milk-guzzling Americans and Europeans who develop osteoporosis, not the rice-and-vegetable eating Chinese.

Calcium is not an unmixed blessing. More is not necessarily better than less. There are numerous degenerative diseases that are characterized by the pathological deposition of calcium in the tissues. Arthritis is accompanied by calcium deposits in the joints. In cataracts, there is a pathological deposition of calcium in the lens of the eye. Calcium kidney stones are quite common, as are calcium gallstones. Arteriosclerosis involves the deposition of calcium in the normally soft and compliant arteries. Calcium deposits are involved with wrinkling and aging of the skin, frozen shoulder, tendinitis, bursitis, heel spurs, otosclerosis (which leads to deafness), and valvular degeneration of the heart. When you put extra calcium in your body, what makes you so sure that it will wind up in your bones? There are plenty of other places for it to go. The popular practice of taking large amounts of calcium pills is an exercise in wishful thinking. There is no guarantee that it will prevent osteoporosis, and it may encourage pathological calcinosis.

Fish eating is the latest craze. The price of fish skyrocketed when it was discovered that there are certain fatty acids in fish that can reduce the tendency of blood to clot. Actually, the high levels of eicosapantanoic acid (EPA) and other omega^3 fatty acids in fish are not fundamentally nutritional. They are not used by the body in a normal, physiological way. They are pharmacological substances, that is, drugs. They interfere with the normal mechanisms involved with blood-clotting. That is why fish oils make people more susceptible to strokes. Taking fish oils does not enhance nutrition, rather, it interferes with it. In any case, it is virtually impossible to have a deficiency of essential fatty acids because they are plentiful and widely distributed in plant foods. A lack of fish oil is not the cause of pathological blood clots. Furthermore, the same fish that are high in EPA are also loaded with saturated fat and cholesterol. You pay a high price for the dubious benefits of taking fish oil.

Egg yolks are high in saturated fat, and each one contains 250 mg. of cholesterol. Who really needs them? Egg whites are hard to digest, and they contain a toxic protein called avidin. Biotin deficiency is produced in animals by feeding them raw egg whites. Eggs, like milk, are among the most allergenic foods. Increasingly today, eggs are likely to be contaminated with salmonella. There is really no good reason to eat them.

Whole, natural, plant foods, eaten both raw and conservatively cooked, are best. You will thrive eating fresh fruits, crisp, green salads, steamed vegetables, baked potatoes, brown rice, red lentils and other nourishing plant foods. The only nutritional question mark on such a diet would be Vitamin B-12.

Vitamin B-12, known as cobalamin, is a very unique nutrient. It is the only cobalt-containing organic compound in nature. It is not produced by animals; it is not produced by plants; it is not produced by people. It is produced only by bacteria. The cow, the horse and the goat are amply supplied with Vitamin B-12 by bacteria inhabiting their digestive tracts. But, humans have fewer B-12 producing bacteria than these animals, and they do not absorb B-12 as readily. Furthermore, we wash and scrub and peel everything until there are no bacteria left on the food. As a result, it is not unusual to find low serum levels of Vitamin B-12 among vegetarians. We can speculate that if Man lived in a state of nature and ate his unwashed food directly from the soil, as the animals do, he would never develop a Vitamin B-12 deficiency. But under modern conditions, the only way we can be sure of maintaining an adequate Vitamin B-12 level on a vegetarian diet is to take a Vitamin B-12 supplement. One good option is to take 1 Twin Labs Vitamin B-12 "dot" per week. But, keep in mind, that this is the only real weak spot in a whole foods vegetarian diet.

Every other vitamin, mineral and amino acid can be readily obtained from a diet of whole, unprocessed, plant foods.

There is no good reason for you to join the vitamin brigade. Notwithstanding the hundreds, if not thousands, of books available, urging you to "boost your energy, " "enhance your immune system, " "heighten your sexuality" and "extend your life span" by taking vitamins, there is virtually no proof to support these exorbitant claims. Not a single human life has ever been "extended" by taking mega-vitamins (except where there have been frank deficiencies to begin with). The claims of the vitamin pundits are based mostly upon animal experiments under laboratory conditions, which cannot be extrapolated to human conditions. Vitamin therapy is just another pie-in-the sky promotion, designed to separate you from your money. In fact, the sale of vitamin pills is the biggest commercial health racket of all time.

There is no business more profitable than the sale of vitamins, and money is the reason behind the hoopla about vitamins. Take the money out of vitamins, and they would practically disappear overnight. Imagine a product: that has a long shelf-life, that requires no refrigeration, that can be easily stored and transported, that can be marked up by more than 100%, that promises to do everything, but that can be held to do practically nothing, and you will have a pretty good picture of what vitamin sales are all about. Is it any wonder that the vitamin industry is such a crowded field? Books and magazines touting vitamins sell swiftly because people are attracted to anything that promises fast and easy solutions to age-old problems. Pop a few vitamins, and slow down the aging process. Take a few vitamins, and cancel out the ill-effects of your bad habits. Swallow a few pills, and revive a declining sex life. Take vitamins as an antidote to stress and pollution. But, what they don't tell you, is that vitamins, in the context of pills, are pharmacological substances, that is - drugs. Vitamin therapy is a form of drug therapy. Taking mega-vitamins is not only habit-forming; it can be physically and psychologically addicting. Consider the typical scenario of a person taking vitamins. He starts off with a multiple tablet, but as he keeps reading about the wonders of vitamins, he adds some extra C and B complex. But, then he wants extra calcium for his bones, more E and zinc to boost his sex drive and a little extra A so that he can see better at night. He keeps reading, and he learns all about free radicals and the need for antioxidants, and before long he is taking huge doses of selenium, a trace element that can be highly toxic, and BHT, a food preservative. At this point, he is taking enough pills, powders and potions to sink a battleship.

No one was ever meant to live that way! The human race has sustained itself on Earth, *eating food* for over a million years, and now we are being told that it is impossible to be well- nourished unless we dose ourselves with large amounts of synthetic vitamins. To those who would enslave people to a lifetime of incessant pill-popping, I would remind them that the human body is not a chemistry set and you are not supposed to play with it, tinker with it or conduct experiments on it. Assaulting the body with a hodge-podge of vitamins, minerals and exotic anti-oxidants is a dangerous and uncertain experiment. I don't think that there is any such thing as "life-extension," but I know very well that there is such a thing as life-shortening. Rather than trying to slow down the aging process by taking pills, it would be far better if people would just stop all the things that accelerate aging (such as eating high-fat, high-protein diets, consuming too many calories, being inactive, drinking alcohol, smoking tobacco, taking drugs and getting too much sun). We do not have to turn our lives into a complicated, pharmacological undertaking in order to be healthy.

Today's vitaminizing revolves mostly around the "free radical theory of aging." According to this theory, the great culprit, the cause of all our troubles, is the sea of oxygen that we live in. Although oxidation is the very means by which we extract energy from food, there is also a down side to oxygen. As a result of these oxidations, hyperactive molecules, like hydrogen peroxide, are formed which can damage tissues. Theoretically, we can enhance the neutralization of these free radicals by taking large doses of Vitamin C, Vitamin E, selenium and other things.

Consider how far we've come. It used to be that we sought remedies only to treat disease. Now the very nature of life on Earth is being seen as a pathological problem in need of a cure.

You cannot go to war with your *existence*, and that is exactly what these "life-extension" pundits are trying to do. It is one thing to try to understand how life processes work so as to better meet the requirements of life and to better harmonize with the nature of life. It is something else to attack and try to change the most basic and fundamental processes of life.

We are oxygen-breathing creatures, and there is nothing we can do to change that. If we had evolved on another planet with a different atmosphere, perhaps our biochemistry would have taken a different route. But, we are what we are, and we had better make our peace with that. There is nothing wrong with trying to minimize destructive oxidations by avoiding excesses. If awareness of the free radical theory of aging prompts you to eat less fat, that could be good. But, the minute you start dosing yourself with huge doses of antioxidants, you embark upon the most grandiose and speculative therapeutic trial ever conducted. You cannot treat basic life processes as a problem in need of a remedy without turning your whole life into one giant, non-stop, therapeutic trial. What can be the outcome of such a venture? If widespread and unpredictable havoc can result from relatively minor dosing, what "side effects" can we look forward to when life itself becomes the disease being treated?

We have to learn to work with life processes, and not against them. Oxidative processes are not a recent development. They have been part and parcel of life, if not from the beginning, certainly from very early in the game. Human beings have always handled oxygen by means of the natural and normal biochemical mechanisms with which we are all endowed, and there is no reason why we cannot do the same today. The presence of pollution on the Earth is no justification for adopting hair-brain, therapeutic schemes. You and I have just as many opportunities to make healthful choices today as anyone else who lived previously.

Let your body use the antioxidants that are naturally present in balanced form in whole foods to deal with oxygen. Don't tamper with a system that has been working beautifully and successfully for millions upon millions of years. There is nothing fundamentally wrong with the way life works. This ocean of air that we live in is, and always has been, our home. And, despite what the pundits say, we are perfectly adapted to it.

Your health is not something with which to speculate. I marvel that people who would never speculate with their money, will try anything when it comes to their health. The wilder and more unorthodox it is, the better. When it comes to your health, play it safe. Err on the side of caution. Don't gamble with the most precious possession you have - your health.

Vitamins are chemical tools that your body uses. The key word here is "*uses*". Vitamins do not act on the body; *the body acts on the vitamins*. Your body *uses* vitamins to process the carbohydrates, fats and proteins in foods, and it uses them in the ratios and proportions in which they are found within natural foods. Vitamins are co-enzymes that combine with larger molecules known as apo-proteins to form whole enzymes. Since the production of apo-proteins is rigidly controlled by the body, taking extra vitamins (above physiological norms) cannot boost the production of active biological substances. Remember, the biological activity is of the whole enzyme, not just the vitamin. In other words, even if a vitamin does have the ability to stimulate a particular pathway, it is not going to reach the final product anyway. Megavitamins do not function as vitamins at all. Instead they clutter the tissues with the intermediary products of metabolism that can accelerate aging. Juggling your body chemistry by taking huge amounts of vitamins is a fool's gamble; it is more likely to do harm than good. There is nothing to be gained by taking vitamins in amounts greater than the body can use them, and there is something to lose — the physiological expenditure involved with excreting them. The net effect of taking megavitamins is to produce an expensive and exotic urine, and to overwork the liver and kidneys. Despite the claims of the vitamin pundits, your body seeks immediately to expel an excess of vitamins. You are going to war with your body when you attempt to "saturate" it with mega-vitamins. Vitamins are nutrients, not remedies. They are food factors, not antidotes for stress or pollution. Rather than extend your life, you are more likely to expend your life, processing commercial vitamins.

It is often stated that because our foods are grown with chemical fertilizers on depleted soils and shipped long distances, that we are likely to be shortchanged when we rely upon commercial produce. There is much exaggeration in this argument. The amount of vitamins contained in a food is determined by the genetics of the plant, not by the type of fertilizer used. If a food is reasonably fresh and agreeable in taste and appearance, you can be certain that it contains an abundance of vitamins, regardless of how it was grown. Plants need vitamins for their growth and development, just as people do. In order to reach maturity and acquire all of the characteristics it has of color, texture, flavor and aroma, a plant must manufacture the full complement of vitamins that it needs. The good news is that organically grown foods are becoming more widely available. They cost a little more, but they're worth it to avoid pesticide exposure.

It's funny how we never wonder if, as a result of modern agricultural practices, tobacco plants still produce nicotine, or whether coffee beans still contain caffeine, or whether coca leaves still have cocaine, but we worry about whether oranges still produce Vitamin C. Rest assured that it is just as necessary for oranges to contain Vitamin C, as it is for marijuana plants to contain the drug, THC.

The situation in regard to minerals is much the same. Plants need minerals like calcium, phosphorus, magnesium, potassium and iron in order to grow. There are only a few trace elements that people require that plants do not. But, the trace mineral content of soils varies widely. By eating a wide variety of foods grown in different regions, trace mineral nutrition can be assured. This is easier to do than you might think. Walk into any well-stocked supermarket, and you are likely to find bananas from Ecuador, oranges from California, papayas from Hawaii, potatoes from Idaho, mangos from Mexico, grapes from Chili, grapefruit from Florida and watermelon from Texas. Trace mineral deficiencies are more likely to occur in remote, rural areas than in big cities where foods are coming in from all over. Eating a wide variety of whole, natural foods is the safest and most certain way of obtaining the right balance of minerals.

This issue concerning the alleged nutritional inadequacy of modern commercial produce is more of a theoretical problem than a demonstrable fact. But, for those who are concerned about it and who insist on taking something for insurance, my advice would be to take a low dose vitamin/mineral supplement, such as NuVeg Daily Multi (take one daily, not four as listed). This product is reasonably balanced and it is assembled from non-animal sources. Even its capsule is made from plant fibers instead of from gelatin, which is something that vegetarians appreciate. Those taking this product have no need to take additional Vitamin B-12; there is an ample amount in it. You should be especially wary of taking vitamin products that contain high levels of fat-soluble vitamins A and D. Also you should be wary of taking high doses of iron. If you are not pregnant or anemic, you have no need for extra iron, which is plentiful in food. The beauty of plant food is that it provides sufficient iron without fostering iron overload, as does meat. Today, the danger of iron toxicity is becoming increasingly recognized. Blood-letting is making a comeback as a medical treatment because it is the most simple and efficient way to remove excess iron from the body.

The most important concept in nutrition is balance — not the balance in a food or the balance in your diet — but the balance inside of you. Your body goes to great lengths to establish and maintain the proper balance of nutrients within your blood. No food or combination of foods is perfectly suited to your body's needs. Therefore, there is always some challenge to your body's delicate balance whenever food is eaten. But, when we dose ourselves with huge amounts of vitamins we greatly magnify the body's nutritional stress. The body has to do more work, and expend more energy, in getting rid of vitamins. The benefits of doing it are only theoretical; they have never been proven. But, the hazards are well known. I advise you to save your money and use it to buy the choicest fruits, vegetables, grains and legumes available. That way, you are sure to get real value for your money, and you will be building your health with certainty.

* * * * * *

You will find that when you eat Hygienically, you require less water than otherwise. This is because raw fruits and vegetables provide a great deal of water, and because a low-salt, low-protein, vegetarian diet occasions less thirst. Do not feel compelled to force down eight glasses of water each day. Excess water drinking can be harmful because it overworks the kidneys and bloats the tissues. Under most circumstances, you should simply drink according to thirst. Only under extreme conditions of strenuous activity in hot weather should it be necessary to drink water copiously.

The water you drink should be the cleanest and purest available — nothing but H_2O. It is much better to rely on unprocessed plant foods as a source of minerals, than to rely on any kind of water. Most, if not all, of the minerals in water are toxic to humans. The best methods of water purification are steam distillation and reverse osmosis. When you get used to drinking water that is really clean, you will no longer be able to tolerate the foul and earthy taste of mineralized water. And, drinking tap water will become completely impossible. You'll gag on the stuff. I keep a carbon filter attached to my kitchen spout to improve the quality of the water with which I wash my foods.

Water is the solvent of life. It is the liquid in which all of the processes of nutrition and drainage take place within your body. Don't settle for anything less than totally pure water.

* * * * * *

Physical activity is no less important than diet to your health and well being. Exercise can actually strengthen your resolve to overcome bad habits, because the discipline needed to train can spill over into other areas of your life and increase your self-control. As your body takes shape, and your conditioning improves, you will naturally tend to move away from destructive practices that sabotage your fitness efforts.

Just about any kind of exercise is good. The most important criterion is that you enjoy it. Your exercise has got to be more than just a health discipline. It must have true recreational value, providing a release from the stress and tension that affect your life otherwise. You should feel good after a workout, a bit winded and tired perhaps, but relaxed and psychologically renewed. Have fun when you exercise. If you play tennis or golf, don't take the game so seriously that you get frustrated and keyed up every time you miss a shot. Keep your priorities straight: you are out there to get some fresh air and physical activity and to have fun — not to do an imitation of John McEnroe.

The regularity of doing exercise is more important than the intensity when it comes to determining the health benefits. As long as you vary the kind of exercise you do, there is no reason why you cannot exercise every day. On the other hand, take a complete day of rest once a week, and whenever you feel especially sore or tired. You don't have to go to extremes in order to derive all of the benefits that exercise can give. Thirty minutes a day of continuous activity will fully provide all of the cardiovascular benefits.

According to Dr. Kenneth Cooper, of Aerobics fame, anyone who runs more than three miles per day, is doing it for something other than health and cardiovascular fitness. This is a startling admission, considering that Dr. Cooper, himself, is a marathon runner. But, you don't have to be a marathon runner or an Ironman triathlete in order to be fit and healthy. The concept of moderation applies just as much to exercise as it does to food. Enjoy exercise, but don't become addicted to it. Exercise should be only a source of joy and happiness in your life, not a source of frustration and anxiety. Keep it fun.

Favor exercises that get your whole body moving in a fluid and natural way, such as brisk walking, cycling and swimming. The best place to exercise is outside in the open air (assuming that the air is fit to breathe). Get involved with more than one activity. Varying your exercise prevents boredom and staleness, while it reduces the likelihood of injury. Be gradual in your transitions from rest to activity, that is, warm up and cool down. Don't become obsessed with exercise, but do fall in love with it. Exercise should be one of the greatest joys in your life, not a bitter pill to swallow. If you don't enjoy your exercise and look forward to it each day, keep searching. You obviously haven't found the activity that suits you best, the one that you could enjoy for a lifetime, even if it didn't promise health benefits. There are enough things in life that you have to do. Exercise should be something that you *love* to do.

Remember that the flip side of exercise is rest. The actual building and strengthening and renovating of the body takes place during rest and sleep, when growth and nutritional processes are at their maximum. Get plenty of sleep at night, and don't hesitate to take a midday nap when circumstances permit. The way to determine whether you are getting enough rest and sleep in your life is to examine how you feel first thing in the morning. Do you wake up spontaneously, feeling refreshed, without having to rely on an alarm clock? Do you make the transition from sleep to wakefulness rapidly and easily? Do you feel prepared for physical and mental activity without resorting to coffee and other stimulants? Do you wake up with a positive mental attitude? If your answer to any of these questions is, "No", then you are probably not getting enough sleep. Why not go to bed earlier each night and sleep in on the weekends? I learned a long time ago to make sleep a priority in my life, and I am certain that it has done more to increase my energy than any other single thing.

But, whatever you do, don't resort to taking sleeping pills of any kind. You cannot induce sleep with drugs. The only drug-induced states are stupor, coma, narcosis and anesthesia, none of which is equivalent to sleep. Don't confuse sleep with drug-induced unconsciousness. The former is a normal, physiological state, in which the body is at peace, and during which the internal processes of repair and recuperation are at their maximum. The latter is a disturbed, pathological state in which the body is engaged in a life and death struggle with a poison. As far as I am concerned, taking sedatives is a pernicious practice, with or without medical approval.

* * * * * *

The last element of Hygiene that I wish to discuss is sunlight. I realize that the sun has received a lot of bad press lately. Certainly, the medical profession has had nothing good to say about it, especially the dermatologists. But, just because someone drowned in the lake, is no reason to condemn swimming. An excess of sunlight will most certainly do harm, but a reasonable and moderate amount of it can do much good. It is no exaggeration to say that sunlight has enormous benefits to health. It naturally tends to lower blood pressure, strengthen the heart, lower cholesterol, stabilize the blood sugar and increase energy, endurance and muscular strength (from *Sunlight* by Zane Kime, M.D.). Sunlight increases our resistance to infection, and it enhances our production of hormones. Granted, there have been studies showing a connection between sunlight and skin cancer. But, a study by Dr. Frank Apperly showed that overall cancer deaths in the United States and Canada were inversely proportional to the amount of sunlight received. In other words, the more sunlight, the less cancer.

Everyone knows that sunlight activates the production of Vitamin D in the skin. But, did you know that it is cholesterol that your body converts into Vitamin D? In other words, the more Vitamin D formed in your skin from exposure to sunlight, the more cholesterol your body uses up.

Many people today prefer to obtain their Vitamin D from pills or from "fortified" foods. But, there may be danger in this, because Vitamin D is actually a steroid hormone, and it can be quite toxic. Yet, it takes only a few minutes of direct exposure to sunlight each day to protect against Vitamin D deficiency. The body cannot overproduce Vitamin D from sunlight. It has a clever scheme of not completely activating the Vitamin D molecule that is made under the sun's influence until it is really needed. Vitamin D can be stored in the liver in large amounts and for long periods of time, so you don't have to worry about a deficiency occurring because of cloudy spells.

So, don't be afraid to get a little sunshine. Just be careful about it. If you are going to be out in the sun for a long time, you should use a sunscreen. It is far better, however, to limit your exposure than to rely on such chemicals. If you know that your skin is very sensitive to the sun, start with just 2 or 3 minutes at a time. Never allow yourself to get red, or even to develop a dark tan, because these are indications of skin damage.

One of the first things you discover in life is that sunshine feels good on your body. If you enjoy the sun moderately and carefully, I believe it will only boost your health.

* * * * * *

What does it mean to live Hygienically? It means to partake of all the truly good things in life and to avoid all the harmful ones. It means to seek out and eat the most wholesome food that you can obtain. It means to treat food for what it is: *raw material for the body's use* — nothing more and nothing less. Food is not a remedy, not a cure, nor is it any kind of specific. We eat for general nourishment and not for any other specific effects. Whatever specific effect a food may have is likely to be bad, because that effect would indicate some kind of disturbance. When a food is eaten and then perfectly digested, absorbed and assimilated, it occasions no disturbance, and hence, it has no specific effect. Rather, it occasions only a *general* sense of well-being.

As a Hygienist, I know that the energy that I have at this moment is not derived from my last meal; rather, it is the manifestation of my general health, which itself is the product of all the behaviors that have characterized my life over the weeks, months and years that have brought me to this moment. I enjoy food, but I am also free of it. I know that I can eat lunch or not eat lunch and still feel good that afternoon. Without eating, my body will simply marshal the internal, nutritive resources that it has in great abundance. In the long run, I am dependent upon food, but I never have to worry about it in the course of my life. From day to day, my body is nutritionally self-sufficient. Never do I have to look for anything to give me energy; I generate my own. Never do I have to resort to biologically foreign substances to maintain my health; I have no need for them and my body cannot use them.

I exercise, not because I have to, but because it feels good to set by body in motion and to feel the energy effortlessly flowing through my muscles. I want to move the way an animal moves: fluidly, with complete ease and balance, and with all parts of my body in complete harmony and accord.

The Hygienic life is truly the good and joyous life. In Hygiene, becoming healthy is not a separate thing that you do, or have done to you; rather, it is the result of the total process by which you live your life. Hygiene removes encumbrances and complications from your life, while it simplifies your needs and wants. A good health program should reduce the hassles and bothers in your life - not give you new ones to worry about. A good health program should set you free from therapeutic dependency - not tie you down to new and "alternative" treatments. Natural Hygiene gives your body its one best chance of finding that delicate state of balance toward which it is always working.

Feasting on luscious fruits and vegetables, imbibing pure, clean water, basking moderately in the sunshine, using the body with freedom and expansion in joyous activity, and securing plenty of rest and sleep may seem like a life of asceticism to some. But, you'd be surprised how fast it grows on you.

A list of organizations is provided in Appendix I.

CHAPTER 7

HOW FOOD ADDICTIONS ARE DIFFERENT

The more deeply the path is etched, the more it is used, and the more it is used, the more deeply it is etched.

— *Jo Coudert*

More than alcohol, more than tobacco, and more than coffee, food addictions are the hardest ones to break. In fact, your battle with food may well be a lifelong struggle. Alcohol, tobacco and coffee are poisons, and your body has a natural aversion to them. Abstinence and healthful living restore that natural aversion to where you don't have to say "NO" anymore! Your body does it for you! Live Hygienically for a year and abstain from tobacco, and you will be no more inclined to smoke cigarettes than to stick your head into a chimney. Live Hygienically and abstain from alcohol for a year, and you will be no more inclined to drink alcohol than to drink paint thinner. Live Hygienically and abstain from coffee for a year, and you will be no more inclined to drink coffee than to drink mud. *But,* live Hygienically and abstain from ice cream for a year, and a bowl of ice cream may still look pretty good to you. Unless you are allergic to it, your body does not have a natural aversion to ice cream. You can feed it to a newborn baby, whose instincts are not depraved, and he or she will relish it. But try to feed the baby coffee or alcohol, and you will have a fight on your hands. The unconditioned organism swiftly and unequivocally says "NO!" to outright poisons.

Unfortunately, when it comes to food, it really is not hard to fool Mother Nature. Our cooks, chefs and food processors have become highly adept at preparing tasty dishes that cause all kinds of trouble inside the body, but which trigger no alarms or cries of protest, at the outset. Of course, over time you can regain your appreciation for unprocessed, natural foods and enjoy them immensely, but don't expect to be repulsed by ice cream anytime soon.

Your fight against food addictions is largely intellectual. You can't count on your instincts to win the battle for you. You have to beat food addictions with your mind. Apply the five step Quit for Good Program. You can either direct your avoidance to individual foods (like ice cream) or to categories of foods (like desserts), whichever is more appropriate to your situation.

Remember that your sense of taste is a relative thing. Something is sweet or sour or salty or bland in comparison to something else.

When my son was small, he enjoyed feeding carrots to the horses. The owner would tell us that we had no idea what a treat it was for the horses to get the carrots. The rest of their diet was so dry and bland that to get something as sweet and succulent as a carrot was really special. Yet, most people regard carrots as being plain and ordinary and not very special, because of all the other rich foods they are accustomed to eating. Perhaps if they had nothing to eat but hay and fodder for a few weeks, a carrot would seem pretty special to them, too.

Eating and enjoying unprocessed, natural foods would be the easiest thing in the world if that were all that people had to eat. For instance, you could prepare yourself a nice meal at home of salad, vegetables and potatoes and eat it with great gusto. But, eat the same meal in a restaurant next to someone who was eating "rich" food, and you would likely feel deprived. That is why limiting your exposure to the bad foods is so important. Out of sight, out of mind.

Perhaps the biggest problem in connection with food is over-eating. The harm over-eating does goes far beyond gaining weight. Over-eating abuses the stomach, and it is the chief cause of indigestion. Over-eating encourages fermentation and putrefaction of food in the digestive tract, which produces gas and discomfort. Over-eating at night impairs sleep. Over-eating on proteins overworks the liver and kidneys. Over-eating on fats increases the viscosity of the blood, impairs circulation, and can raise serum cholesterol and triglycerides. Over-eating on carbohydrates, particularly when they are refined, can cause havoc with your blood sugar.

A high calorie intake, besides making you fat, accelerates the aging process. Dr. Ray Wolford, chief Gerontologist at UCLA and author of *The 20 Year Diet*, has said that the only thing that has been found to consistently increase the life span of animals is food restriction. Not extra vitamins or minerals or antioxidants, but rather caloric restriction has proved to be the one true "Fountain of Youth." Moderation in eating is, therefore, important to everyone, not just those who are overweight.

Over-eating also encourages you to make the wrong food choices. It ruins your natural hunger for unprocessed foods, so that all you want is something sweet or something salty. You have to be genuinely hungry to enjoy apples, celery, lettuce and carrots. But, ice cream would taste good whether you were hungry or not.

We tend to think of hunger as a bad thing. It brings images to mind of starving Ethiopians and concentration camp victims. We forget that hunger is a normal part of human life. Hunger is how your body tells you that it wants food. Hunger is what imparts deliciousness to food. The disappearance of hunger is what tells you that you've had enough food. If we never give ourselves a chance to experience hunger, we are silencing an important feedback mechanism that was meant to serve us on a daily basis.

Do an experiment and start paying close attention to your state of hunger. Don't just eat at mealtime because the clock has struck a certain hour. Ask yourself whether you are truly hungry. And if you are not truly hungry, wait a while. Let your hunger grow and develop until there is no question in your mind that it's there. Try to distinguish between hunger and appetite. Hunger is a general desire for food, accompanied by a watering of the mouth, a heightening of taste and smell and a sense of anticipation about eating. Hunger is not persnickety; almost any wholesome food will do. The more hungry you are, the less finicky you become about food. Appetite is the desire for a particular food, often in the absence of true hunger. If you are hungry for just one thing, and nothing else will do, you may not be hungry at all. Hunger is like thirst in that it is a mouth and throat sensation. It should not be accompanied by abdominal pain, headache or any other discomfort. Hunger can be a positive emotional state when one has the expectation of eating. Weakness is not the primary manifestation of hunger (although, granted, one will eventually become weak from a lack of food). Remember that even animals in the wild have to work for their food, and were they to become weak at the first sign of hunger, they would hardly be able to hunt or forage.

When hungry, you celebrate the coming food. It would be no fun to eat if you never became hungry. Feeding yourself would be no different from filling your gas tank. So, don't be afraid of hunger. Tuning in to hunger is what enables you to pilot yourself to moderation in eating.

Most people blame hunger for making them overweight, but hunger is not the cause of it. The problem is with the foods that people select to satisfy their hunger. It is natural and normal to want to eat until you feel satisfied. But, if most or all of the foods you eat are refined, processed and concentrated, you don't stand a chance. In order to eat enough quantity to feel satisfied, you have to over-eat. That is why if you are overweight, you should plan all of your meals around high-fiber, water-sufficient foods, namely, the juicy fruits and succulent vegetables. You can fill up on these foods without getting an excess of calories. You don't have to deprive yourself. It is much easier to place restrictions on what you eat, than on how much you eat. There are probably already things that you don't eat, so if you add a few more things to the list, you will not be starting a new trend. The idea is to allow yourself to eat freely of whole, natural foods so that you don't have to struggle with amounts. You can lose a lot of weight that way without suffering.

Snacking is a pernicious habit. I call it the "One-Meal-a-Day Plan." It lasts from the moment you wake up in the morning, until the time you go to bed at night. Snacking not only encourages you to over-eat, but it also undermines your digestion. I think it is best to avoid eating between meals and especially late at night. You will enjoy your food more if you allow your hunger to build between meals.

If you tend to over-eat, try assembling your whole meal before you start eating it, just as you would do in a cafeteria. Put together what you think would be a reasonable platter of food; and commit yourself to eating that amount, and no more, before you take your first bite. Then, you can just relax and enjoy your food, knowing that you have decided in advance not to over-eat. Focus on foods that have to be chewed. Part of the satiation from eating comes from the time it takes to hold the food in your mouth and prepare it for swallowing. When your diet consists of blends, drinks, soups, gruels and puddings, you have to consume more to get the same amount of satisfaction. Don't look for ways to make your food easier to eat. Eat it the old-fashioned way: CHEW IT!

If you lose your hunger for natural foods, the best thing to do is to fast. Rather than look for ways to jazz up your diet with condiments and dressings, just miss a few meals. As they say, "Hunger is the best sauce". And there is no better way to restore a natural hunger for real food than by fasting. Try to rest and relax as much as possible on your fast day. A brief fast is not only safe, it's good for you. It gives your stomach and intestines a rest. It promotes detoxification, and it restores your desire for wholesome food. So if you can't decide what you want to eat, perhaps your decision should be not to eat at all. Of course, anyone with significant health problems should seek the advice of a doctor who is knowledgeable about fasting before doing it.

Your battle with food may be a lifelong struggle, but with the Quit for Good Program and a Hygienic diet, you are bound to succeed. Don't be tempted to use commercial weight loss powders. They are definitely the wrong means to achieve your end. These powders provide exactly what you don't need — refined and processed calories. The first ingredient listed on the container of such products is sugar! In fact, these products are quite similar in composition to other formulas that are intended to promote weight gain. The main difference is that they are lower in calories. But, that is a function mostly of dilution, and it does not change the fundamental nature of the product or the effect it has upon metabolism. Weight loss resulting from the use of these products is almost always temporary, because the rebound tendency to gain weight afterwards is so great.

A diet for weight loss should be completely vegetarian. There is no good reason to include animal foods. Fresh juicy fruits, crisp succulent vegetables, and unrefined starches such as potatoes, yams and brown rice are the best choices. Fats and oils of all kinds should be eliminated, and it is also wise to stay away from breads and other flour products. If you feel that you absolutely must have bread, make it the Essene bread, because it contains only sprouted wheat and water. Even this should be eaten sparingly by those trying to lose weight. Most slenderizing of all are green salads. Of course you must avoid oily dressings. A few mild seasonings, some green onions, mixed together with lemon juice or a splash of apple cider vinegar is all it takes to put pizazz in your salad.

So, in trying to lose weight, the best exercise is to push the grocery cart straight to the fruit and vegetable section of your supermarket and load it up with melons, apples and potatoes. Granted, fresh produce has become increasingly expensive. There are few items that are cheap anymore. But just think of the enormous health benefits that come from eating these foods, and think also of the many ways you can save money by adopting a Hygienic way of life. Think of all the things you do not have to buy once you begin to live Hygienically. Your savings on doctor bills alone should more than compensate for what you have to spend on food. When you take everything into account, living Hygienically is, by far, the most economical thing you can do.

CHAPTER 8

QUIT FOR GOOD: A TOOL FOR PERSONAL GROWTH

Mind is the master power that molds and makes,
And man is mind, and evermore he takes
    the tool of thought,
And shaping what he wills,
Brings forth a thousand joys, a thousand ills:
He thinks in secret, and it comes to pass:
Environment is but his looking-glass.

— *James Allen*

Overcoming bad habits is really a part of a larger process of becoming free from constraints and dependencies, which you have been doing your whole life. Getting free has been your mission in life. You were born into the world a totally helpless and dependent being. The only thing you could do for yourself was breathe. All of your other needs had to be provided by others. But, one step at a time, you learned to do things for yourself. Overcoming dependency has been the goal of your development and the mark of your maturity. It is also what enables you to feel good about yourself.

Constructive learning always involves personal growth. Your capacity to do something new, not only widens the choices of action you have, but it gives you more personal control of your environment and your life. But, this personal expansion applies just as much to "non-doing" as it does to "doing". Being able to say "NO" to a possibility exhibits just as much personal power as the ability to say "YES". When you liberate yourself from a

105

destructive habit, you grow as a person. Your consciousness is raised because you are no longer fixed by the dull, redundant drone of a bad habit.

Alcohol, tobacco and drugs are unmitigated evils. Each one weighs you down, like an albatross around your neck. They poison your body. They impair your mind. They weaken your will. They damage your nerves. They take the joy out of living. Continuously craving a drink or a cigarette is a desperate state to be in. Happiness is not born of such desperation. All of the real pleasures in life are compromised by the desire for such things.

Getting free from a poison habit not only removes a destructive influence from your life, but it also raises your whole level of sensory awareness. When you quit such a habit, your capacity to *feel* increases. You begin to appreciate the taste of real food again. You begin to enjoy the exhilaration of physical activity again. You begin to relate to people more genuinely and attentively. Even love and sex can be sweeter and more satisfying without the stultifying effects of a poison habit. Remove the poison yoke from around your shoulders and you become more light, more free, more balanced and more resilient.

The Quit for Good Program is a way for you to say "NO" to the tyranny of your own bad habits. And, saying "NO" to yourself is harder than saying "NO" to anyone else. But, like most things in life, the longer you do it and the more you practice it, the better you become at it. Over time, you become more and more the master of your own self. Your ultimate goal is to gain control not only of your actions, but also of your reactions. Saying "NO" to habit is the first vital step in the process of controlling your total pattern of response.

You can completely overcome your desire to smoke tobacco. You can completely lose your craving for coffee and other poisons. But, you need a process to initiate those changes, and the Quit for Good Program can be that process. Quit for Good gets you launched. It gets your sails filled with the winds of personal change.

Your behavior at birth was occasioned by an outside stimulus triggering an immediate reflex response. But gradually, that distinctly human interval of thought entered the picture, as a pause between the stimulus and the response. You stopped. You thought. You chose. And in so doing, you began to take control of your own life. Moreover, that chain of events is a process that continues as long as your life goes on. Anytime you *stop* and *think* and *choose*, you exercise the most pivotal human faculty you have: the capacity to reason. This is the power that enables you to act decisively and effectively in pursuit of your own happiness.

The Quit for Good Program enables you to cultivate your reasoning powers in a way that leads to greater awareness and greater personal freedom. By saying "NO" to your own conditioned responses, you open up the door to making significant changes. With the Quit for Good Program, you exercise your power of self-control, meaning in the literal sense, that you build it up and develop it. Just as with physical exercise, you gain strength with each repetition; so, too, with Quit for Good, you gain fortitude with each application. It forces you to confront your bad habit head-on, each and every time the urge for it arises, and it enables you to reaffirm your desire to overcome it, until you do. Quit for Good gives you that steel-eyed focus and determination that you need to win your battle.

Think of the Quit for Good Program as a way for you to resculpt a part of yourself. The "old you" or the "new you"? That is the choice before you. Only you can decide, and only you can make it happen.

GETTING RIGHT IN YOUR BODY

More than anything else, health depends upon the balance inside of you. As a living organism, your body is constantly seeking to maintain and improve its balance. In standing for example, you are never at rest. There is a lot of activity going on to keep yourself upright. Your two feet represent a small platform of support for the body's rather tall column; and with the heavy head on top, there is a lot of leverage at play. Your head is perched on a tiny ring of bone, and it is very easy for your head to fall from there. And, that is exactly what happens. You begin to fall in one direction, and your body compensates by shifting your weight, until you start falling in another direction, which calls for another compensation, and so on and so forth. The net result is a constant state of motion that is so finely tuned that it is hardly noticeable. Only when there is something seriously wrong with your nervous system does this oscillation become apparent. The crucial point is that you don't "do" this balancing. You don't pay attention to the forces at work and make each and every shift yourself. You just direct yourself upward and your body does the rest. You establish an intention, and your body takes care of the details. If you tried to take charge of the mechanism and "do" your own balancing, you would simply fix yourself to the earth and sabotage your mobility. All you can do is establish the right intention and stop interfering with the natural mechanisms that control the whole process.

But, standing upright is not the only balancing act you do. Balance is involved with every aspect of your functioning. For instance, your body is continually adjusting the amount of light entering the eye by contracting and releasing the muscles of the iris that control the size of the pupil. Your body is continually adjusting the activity of the endocrine glands to meet the fluctuating needs of the body for their hormonal secretions. Your body is continually mobilizing and transforming amino acids in order to preserve the nutritional balance of the blood. Your blood chemistry is in a constant state of flux, even when it appears to be stable. Your body is reacting every moment to changes that are occurring both internally and externally.

The activity of the heart is constantly monitored and fine-tuned by the central nervous system in keeping with the fluctuating circulatory needs of the body. Not only your physical activity, but also your mental and emotional activity affect your circulatory requirements. Imagine if it were up to you to speed your heart up every time you hurried up a flight of stairs or witnessed an alarming event. Imagine if you had to slow your heart down each time you attempted to rest. Can you imagine the mess we would get ourselves into if we had to "do" our own circulatory balancing? It is doubtful that we would survive at all. It is a blessing that the body does these things for us.

Most people would agree with the above statements, but for some reason, they do not apply the same reasoning to other aspects of their balance. They want to "do" the balancing of their own blood chemistry. They want to force conditions on the body, such as "vitamin loading" or "vitamin saturation". They think that they know better than the body does, what balance to maintain between the different nutrients and components of the blood. They fail to realize that every time we force a change upon the body, we disturb a crucial and delicate balance. When we supply nutrients to the body with therapeutic force (in the form of mega-vitamins), we are almost always moving further away from a balanced and optimum internal state. This is so, regardless of how they make us feel.

If a person is suffering from alcohol intoxication, he can attempt to correct it by drinking strong coffee. He may seem to improve, but coffee is not an antidote for alcohol, and supplying coffee merely adds a new and different chemical blow to the one that is already present. Now he has two poisons to react to instead of just one. The improvement is really a delusion. The person is actually even further away from a normal, healthy state for having taken the coffee. Taking the coffee merely produces a different kind of abnormality, one which appears to be more acceptable on the surface, but which is certainly not more wholesome underneath. Now the inebriated person must wait for the effects of two drugs to wear off before he can again be normal.

This is a good example of the concept of "end-gaining," which was first described by the Australian movement educator, F. Mathias Alexander. End-gaining refers to the practice of only looking at our goals or objectives, and not at the means that we employ to achieve them. Dr. Wilfred Barlow, a protégé of Alexander defined end-gaining as "action which does not pay heed to the manner of use." Alexander pointed out that our means have consequences of their own, which are often just as penetrating as our ends. We should be just as attentive to our means as to our ends to insure that we do not produce too many harmful side effects in going after what we want. It matters not only what we do, but how we do it. The process is just as important as the final results. The process of overcoming alcohol intoxication depends upon rest and abstinence, and not upon stimulation with coffee or other drugs.

There is a world of difference between stopping something, in order to achieve a certain improvement, and actually doing something or taking something to achieve the improvement. When we stop doing a wrong thing, we remove an impediment, an obstacle to good functioning, and we thereby increase the overall balance and stability of the system. However, when we do something or take something to force a change, we generally de-stabilize the system because the body has to react to everything that is put into it or done to it. We tend to look narrowly at the effects of what we do, rather than at the big picture, with all of its ramifications. That is why it is always safer to stop doing things that are wrong, in order to effect change, rather than to force change directly with end-gaining methods.

The use of prescribed drugs to reduce blood pressure is a good example of end-gaining. High blood pressure is not caused by a lack of drugs, and taking drugs does not correct any of the underlying problems associated with it. Medication merely creates a different kind of abnormal state, one which may mimic a healthy state, but which is never identical to it. Nausea, vomiting, liver damage, kidney failure, cardiac arrhythmias, depression and impotence are among the "side effects" of blood pressure medication. What good is it to "solve" a problem in a way that creates numerous other problems that are as bad as or worse than the original one? It is damnable that people have medications thrust upon them (often for the remainder of their lives), when a few simple life-style changes would correct their high blood pressure, and usually in a matter of weeks. Eliminate the bad diet, the excess weight, the cigarettes, the alcohol and the coffee, and you will see the blood pressure normalize spontaneously. Hypertension is a life-style problem. If you stop causing the problem, it goes away. It requires changes in behavior - not pharmacological intervention.

We all know that "actions have consequences." But we sometimes forget that our actions can have other consequences besides those we are seeking. We may take a huge dose of Vitamin C in order to "increase our resistance" or "bolster our immune system." But, if we look only at those lofty objectives we will ignore the fact that taking Vitamin C also disturbs the pH of the blood, irritates the stomach, increases the production of oxalic acid and uric acid, encourages kidney stones, overloads the body with iron, depletes the body of calcium and has other effects which are clearly undesirable. Such rampant end-gaining sets in motion a vicious cycle of disruption, and it is far more likely to do harm than good.

If people understood how drugs work, I believe they would be less willing to take them. For instance, consider how diuretics work. A diuretic is said to increase urinary output. But, how does it do that? To understand how a diuretic works, you have to understand how the kidneys work. Each kidney consists of about one million individual filters called nephrons. The blood vessels that course through the nephrons have a unique permeability that permits fluid and dissolved particles from the blood to enter special tubules. But, this initial filtrate from the blood is not the finished product that we call urine. As the fluid passes through the long tubules, the body absorbs back some of the fluid and most of the nutrients that are also present. A diuretic works by crippling the kidneys' ability to carry on this reclamation process from the tubules. The result is that the volume of urine increases, but the quality of the urine becomes distinctly abnormal. Now there is a slow and steady leak of potassium and other valuable minerals from the blood. Remember that the function of the kidneys is not only to remove water, but also to conserve valuable nutrients. Diuretics prevent the kidneys' ability to perform this latter process. Does this sound like the kidneys are being strengthened? Does it sound like the function of the kidneys is being improved? Is it worth it to embellish a clinical measurement (in this case, urinary output) by means that destroy healthy functioning? What are the long-term consequences of doing it? There can be no doubt that to ignore the life-style factors that cause kidney sluggishness, and to take diuretics instead, leads ultimately to kidney failure.

You cannot take a situation that is wrong, add another wrong to it, and thereby produce something that is right.

Everyone knows that, in life, two wrongs do not make a right. Yet, few people realize that the same is true regarding health.

Aspirin is recommended today to prevent dangerous blood clots. But, few patients realize that aspirin works by interfering with and disrupting the normal function of the specialized blood cells known as platelets. Your blood needs to have the capacity to clot; otherwise, you would bleed to death from a minor injury. Now you know why aspirin users are subject to sudden hemorrhages.

Beta-blockers, like Inderal, work by crippling the heart's ability to contract. By impairing the contractions of the heart, these drugs reduce the heart's output, and hence relieve chest pain, high blood pressure and other symptoms. But, the result is an unmistakable feeling of weakness, especially when attempting to exercise. Sometimes, the weakening effect upon the heart muscle is severe enough to cause heart failure.

These are all examples of *medical end-gaining*, which is the attempt to bring about specific clinical changes by administering drugs that can only impair functioning overall. End-gaining is the attempt to grab for immediate, short-term results, while ignoring the detrimental, long-term effects of our actions. It is generally a waste of time and money to take medicines, and it can do a colossal amount of harm. The seeming improvements that come from taking drugs are hardly worth the widespread internal havoc that they cause.

Of course, there are times in life when the end-gaining approach is necessary and unavoidable. In an emergency, there may be no time to allow natural processes to bring about a successful resolution to a crisis. In bacterial meningitis, for example, permanent brain damage can occur within hours unless antibiotics are given. In a severe episode of asthma, a person could suffocate to death unless they receive medical treatment. However, just because extraordinary means are required in an emergency, does not legitimize those means under non-emergency conditions. Life is not one long string of emergencies. There is a vast difference between taking a drug to abort an episode of acute glaucoma (which is a true emergency) and taking drugs for the usual cases of high blood pressure, high cholesterol, headaches, arthritis, indigestion, constipation, etc. Masking chronic symptoms with drugs is hardly a constructive thing to do. To the greatest extent possible, we should avoid putting drugs of any kind into our bodies. I wish that adults would be as frightened of taking drugs as children naturally are. Taking drugs is always fraught with danger and harm. Drugs are inherently antagonistic to life, and that is precisely why antibiotics are sometimes effective. Essentially, antibiotics make war on both the microbe and the host, but theoretically, they inflict more harm on the microbe, which enables the body to get the upper hand. Although antibiotics have a legitimate role to play in critical cases of infection, let us not forget that it is the resistance of the individual, as a manifestation of general health, that determines who gets sick from infection and who does not.

In Hygiene, we abandon the "remedy mentality" (except in emergencies and other special situations where such intervention is truly needed). Instead, we seek to remove the causes of disease and to provide the general conditions that favor health-building and recovery. Natural Hygiene is a non-therapeutic approach to health that requires time and patience, but it offers real and lasting benefits. Other systems dabble with symptoms, but Hygiene alone builds vigorous health from the ground up.

Not only do we Hygienists shun conventional medicine most of the time, but we completely reject the unorthodox therapies, such as herbology and homeopathy.

Herbology is the practice of poisoning the sick with toxic plants and weeds. Some of the most virulent poisons known to Man are derived from the plant kingdom. Actually, the herbal practice began as a ceremonial practice, the herbs being used by the "shaman" not to treat disease, but to drive out evil spirits. Medical historians have created and perpetuated the myth that primitive people were pharmacologists, while, in fact, they were practicing their religion.

It is important to know that medicinal herbs are drugs. In fact, many modern medical drugs are purifications and refinements of herbal substances. Salicylic acid, for example, which is commonly known as aspirin, is derived from willow bark. Digitalis, a potent heart stimulant, is derived from the flower, foxglove.

What is the difference between an herb and a medicine? The answer is that with a medicine, the exact dose is precisely known, and hence, its toxic effects can be somewhat accurately predicted. With an herb, the amount of the active ingredient is unknown, and therefore, the strength of the dose can only be guessed at. Furthermore, herbs are unregulated, and likewise, those who prescribe herbs are unregulated. Everything about taking herbs is a big question mark.

Sadly, there are many misguided people who still think that if a poison is wrapped up in a plant, it is harmless, and even beneficial. They continue to embrace this delusion in spite of the fact that many plants are capable of killing outright, for example, hemlock. I knew a young woman who was staying at a health resort in California, who went into the woods to collect herbs, and who mistakenly consumed hemlock. Within minutes, she went into a coma and suffered massive and irreversible brain damage. For years she lived, but only as a vegetable. She was unconscious, and her vital functions were maintained by machines. She finally died without ever coming out of her coma.

The fact that herbs are "natural" is irrelevant. Snake venom, poison ivy and tobacco leaves are perfectly natural, but that does not make them good for us. Not everything that is part of nature is fit for human consumption. A bolt of lightning is natural, too.

Remember that there is a big difference between a nutritional herb (a vegetable) and a so-called medicinal herb (which is a poison). The mere fact that a plant can be used as a medicine is proof positive that it is unfit for consumption as a food. The fact that it occasions resistance and expulsive action on the part of the body is proof that the herb is an irritant and an unwelcome intruder. Instead of digesting and utilizing them as foods, the body throws out "medicinal" herbs, and often with great force. The more powerful the effect that an herb has, the more toxic it is. Remember, it is always the body that acts on the herb, and not vice versa.

Herbal teas contain many potent carcinogens. Those who drink comfrey tea on a regular basis have been shown to have abnormal liver function tests. Comfrey tea had been banned in Canada for that reason, although it is still available in the U.S.; Some herbal teas contain potent nerve toxins, like atropine and scapolamine.

Ginseng is an herb that stimulates the body to produce an abnormally large amount of steroid hormones, like cortisone, which can be very damaging because it inhibits the body's defensive and reparative actions.

All of the objections that pertain to conventional medicine apply equally to herbal medicine. Which is more damaging? Who knows? It would be foolish to dabble with herbal remedies in a true emergency, and in a non-emergency, there would be no need to interfere at all.

Therefore, as I see it, there is no legitimate place for herbal medicine in the intelligent care of the well or the sick. Herbal medicine is based no more on physiology and biology than is witchcraft, and I believe that it should be completely abandoned.

Homeopathy is based on the use of infinitesimally small doses of remedies which at higher doses would produce the same symptoms as the disease being treated. Supposedly, "vital force" is imparted to the diluent by shaking it. The more diluted the solution becomes, if properly shaken, the more potent it becomes. The following excerpt from *Fallacies and Foibles* in Medicine by Peter Skrabanek and James McCormick proves that homeopathy is based on nothing but mysticism. I quote it at length because it states the case against homeopathy so perfectly that I cannot possibly improve upon it. After reading this passage, anyone with a shred of allegiance to truth and realism will not have anything to do with homeopathy, either as a doctor or a patient.

"In Homeopathy, when the twelfth centesimal dilution is reached, known as '12C,' the dilution is 10 to the power of 24. The real meaning of this number is difficult to comprehend. Perhaps the best way to try is with 'Caesar's Last Breath Theorem.' If Caesar's last breath has by now become equally distributed throughout the earth's atmosphere, and considering that the volume of the atmosphere is about 10 to the power of 24 times the capacity of our lungs, then with each breath we take, we inhale a single molecule of Caesar's last breath. But 12C is only the beginning; the most common homeopathic dilution is 30C, a dilution of 10 to the power of 60. This is roughly equivalent to one grain of salt dissolved in a volume of diluent that would fill ten thousand billion spheres, each large enough to enclose the whole solar system. According to one publication, potencies of over 100,000 (or 10 to the power of 200,000) have been used 'successfully.' That such delusions can capture the fancy of thousands of educated men and women, is an indictment of the education provided in some medical schools, or possibly evidence that some minds are congenitally incapable of developing critical faculties.

"Yet in the summer of 1988, *Nature*, perhaps the most prestigious of all scientific journals, published an observation from Professor Jacques Benveniste that seemed to materialize the smile of the homeopathic cat, by claiming that water could 'remember' substances that had once been dissolved in it but were no longer present. There was, however, a precondition. Water would only 'remember' if subjected to vigorous shaking between each homeopathic dilution. Stirring alone was not enough. (Perhaps this is why James Bond had his martinis shaken, not stirred.)

"Although not mentioned in the published article, this study was sponsored by the homeopathic industry. This sensational claim was hailed by homeopaths everywhere as the final 'scientific' vindication of their cherished beliefs. Not surprisingly, the editor of *Nature* was attacked for having published nonsense, and by so doing, giving respectability to such dubious ideas. Summer madness reached new heights of frenzy when the editor of *Nature*, accompanied by an investigating team, including James Randi, a professional magician, and Walter Stewart, who specializes in the detection of scientific fraud, descended upon the French laboratory and asked that the experiments be repeated in their presence. This request was granted, but the original findings were not reproducible in the presence of this team. Within a week, another communication appeared in *Nature*, signed by the editor and his companions, entitled, 'High-dilution Experiments a Delusion.' Further attempts to replicate the water-memory experiments - at Rothschild Hospital in Paris - also failed. This effectively ended the matter as far as the scientific community was concerned.

"Had Professor Benveniste's experiments been reproducible by others, the results for science would have been devastating. The consequence for physics would have been more profound than, say, the discovery that the earth is, after all, flat. Science, as we know it, would have had to be scrapped and rewritten along totally different lines. Homeopathy may be one of medical science's greatest misadventures - a folly so massive it will merit study in itself."

What he is saying here is that if you believe in homeopathy, it would be a contradiction for you to even get in your car and drive somewhere, because the laws of physics and chemistry on which those actions are based would be refuted if homeopathy were true. Homeopathy can only be true in a universe where 2 + 2 = 5, but it is not the universe we live in.

Ask yourself the following questions: "What need of the body is fulfilled by administering a homeopathic remedy?" (Answer: None. It has no such need.) "By means of what capacity does the body *use* a homeopathic remedy?" (Answer: None. It has no such capacity.) "What are the consequences of a deficiency of a homeopathic remedy?" (Answer: None. The body can have no such deficiency.)

Scratch the surface of homeopathy, and all you find underneath is mindless mysticism. Any thinking, rational person will reject it.

My call for a contraction in the whole field of therapeutics applies not only to the various forms of Medicine, but also to my own profession of Chiropractic. An enormous amount of time and money is spent on Chiropractic treatment, but in my view, little of it does any real good. I cannot state strongly enough that the human body has no fundamental need for spinal adjustments. In fact, the joints of the spine are delicate neuromuscular mechanisms, and they were never meant to be thrust upon. I never have my spine adjusted, and I want you to know precisely why.

Most of the lesions that chiropractors treat are considered to be insignificant by orthopedists and neurologists. These "subluxations" can be found on virtually everyone. To establish their significance, one would have to not only demonstrate their presence in disease, but also their absence in health. To my knowledge, no one has ever done that. Chiropractors make hay out of the fact that the human body is not perfectly symmetrical.

When you go to the Chiropractor and receive an adjustment, it feels like a bone is being put back into place. You feel the thrust, you hear the pop, and it can be very exhilarating. But usually, the change in alignment is only momentary. The minute you get up from the table and start moving around, the effect of the adjustment begins to wear off. How can an adjustment hold? There is nothing to hold it. In fact, many chiropractors have abandoned the "bone out of place" mentality. They now declare that their intention is to restore motion to the spine, not to realign it. But here again, the improvement in spinal motion from an adjustment is often just temporary. Moreover, it is generally only the passive range of motion that is increased by an adjustment, not the active range of motion. I believe that receiving adjustments is mostly a conditioning process, and it can quickly develop into a therapeutic habit.

We tend to think of the spine as a column of blocks, which makes it easy to imagine one getting out of place or becoming stuck. But, your spine is a living structure, secured by living tissue. Not only are there ligaments, fascia, and joint capsules to limit and define the relationship between segments, but there is the responsive muscle tissue, which not only permits voluntary movement, but also separates and suspends the segments in order to prevent the kind of friction that can occur in a column of blocks. It is certainly true that many of us tend to become stiff as we age. But, this occurs not because of an inherent need for adjustments, but because we tend to use our spines incorrectly. The stiffness is a habitual quality of our movements. Getting adjusted does not teach us how to use our spines better. The problem is one of maladaptive signals between the mind and the muscles. This we must learn to correct consciously through a process of inhibition and direction. An improvement in self-awareness and self-use is the true passport to spinal health.

Think about what happens when you crack your knuckles. You certainly mobilize the knuckle joint, but It doesn't last very long. Within a short while, it becomes stiff again. The main effect of cracking your knuckles is to develop the nervous habit to do so. Unfortunately, there is no more permanent benefit from back cracking than there is from knuckle cracking, and the potential for harm is much greater. This is because of the proximity of the spinal segments to the spinal cord, the spinal nerves and the vertebral arteries. The spine is strong, but it is also intricate and delicate. You would not adjust a wrist watch with a sledge hammer. Neither was the human spine designed to be handled with sudden force.

The practice of Chiropractic is entirely subjective. There are numerous, in fact, myriad different ways that chiropractors go about it. Most of them use high velocity thrusts, but some use slower and more gentle methods. Some manipulate the neck only, while others manipulate every joint in the body. Some do muscle work, either before or after joint manipulation, while others use electrical modalities. Some use their hands only, while others use small hand-held devices to make the adjustments. The process by which a chiropractor analyzes the spine and gives significance to his findings is completely arbitrary. Whatever method he uses, you can be certain that most of his colleagues would disagree with it. Chiropractic is a veritable hodge-podge of physical, thermal, manual and electrical treatments. If you don't believe me, present yourself as a patient to several different Chiropractors. It is likely that they will all arrive at a different analysis of your problem and recommend a different course of treatment. If you are already a Chiropractic patient, present yourself to another Chiropractor under the guise that you have never received adjustments. It is likely that the second Chiropractor will find numerous faults that the first Chiropractor missed because his criterion for evaluating the spine is different. Which one of them Is right? Who knows? They could both be wrong.

Just imagine that you had a toothache and you went to ten different dentists, and not only could they not agree on which treatment you needed, but they could not even agree on which tooth was impaired. I imagine you would be very hesitant to let any of them go near you with a drill. But, that is exactly the situation that exists within Chiropractic. The difference Is that Dentistry is based on science, whereas Chiropractic is not.

Every true science is tied to reality and grows in a linear direction. The work of each scientist is continuously checked, and either confirmed or discredited by other scientists. The result is that there is a continuous shedding of falsehoods and a continuous building upon truths. It brings about an integration of ideas and a resolution of conflicts when objective and scientific standards are kept. Thus, the factual foundation upon which each science is based continues to expand. But, in Chiropractic, the only foundation is the belief that the nervous system controls the body and that adjusting the spine can remove nerve interference. From that broad sweeping premise, one can go in any direction one wants, and that is exactly what Chiropractors do. Today, there are more conflicts in the practical application of Chiropractic theory than ever before. Science is supposed to resolve discrepancies, but in Chiropractic, the discrepancies just keep growing.

Despite its vagaries, Chiropractic is put forward as a virtual panacea- not as the sole solution to every health problem, but as a fundamental requirement of human life, right up there with air, water and food. A lifelong dependency on Chiropractic is exactly what the profession wishes for us. Within Chiropractic philosophy, there is no model by which a person can avoid the need for adjustments. Subluxations result from any kind of "mechanical, chemical or psychological stress". In other words, just about anything in life can cause a subluxation, and we had better resign ourselves to getting adjustments from the cradle to the grave. This attempt to breed a physical and psychological dependency on Chiropractic is reprehensible in my view.

It is my observation that the people who receive the most adjustments are the ones who are most likely to need them. They are the ones whose spines always seem to "go out". There are plenty of people who go their whole lives without ever thinking such a thing or experiencing such an urge. But, once the idea is instilled in them by a Chiropractor that they need adjustments, it can become an obsession. People become addicted to it. They may even start popping their own necks and backs- a most disturbing sight indeed.

Granted, spinal manipulation sometimes provides relief from pain and discomfort. Applying a force to the spine is one way of changing the "bundle of responses" that comprises the individual . It changes the total pattern of response by adding a new and different stimulus, that occasions a new and different reaction. The force represents a therapeutic diversion that distracts the body and temporarily alters the pattern of symptoms. Applying a force to the spine may cause a sudden stretch in a spastic muscle that induces it to relax. A mobilizing adjustment may cause changes In the fluid dynamics around a joint, and it may alter the activity of the sensory nerves. Applying pressure to a tender point with the thumb or elbow may temporarily desensitize it. Everyone knows from common experience that rubbing a sore spot tends to make it feel better. Manual therapists have numerous ways of doing these things, but they all amount to one form or another of palliation, which can be defined as the process of affording temporary relief without dealing with the causes of a problem.

I am not opposed to trying to provide relief to those who are hurting. But, I think that it should be done gently, without sudden and forceful thrusting. Massage, gentle pressure, light traction, and "contract and relax" procedures are much to be preferred over joint popping, because they are infinitely safer and they are just as likely to be effective.

Looming much larger than the palliative effect of manipulation is the placebo effect, which is the improvement that results from the positive psychology connected with receiving a treatment. The mind is a powerful thing. The expectation of being helped begins to make it happen. Just the act of taking an analgesic tends to relieve pain, regardless of the pharmacological effect of the drug. A slight easing of muscle tension, whether it is accomplished by stroking, rubbing, thrusting or stretching, can be translated into a tremendous amount of placebo effect.

What reinforces the placebo effect of Chiropractic is that it is given and evaluated over time. Patients receive adjustments for weeks and months, and sometimes years. If I tear a muscle, the healing of the injury is a biological process that takes place over time. Whether I am rubbed, prodded, cracked, or popped, it is my body that does the healing. Any time a treatment is given over time, you must ask yourself the following question: "How much of the improvement is due to the passage of time and would have occurred anyway without treatment, given reasonably good conditions?" Healing is spontaneous, and therapeutics receives more credit than it deserves.

Let us consider what happens when you combine a small amount of palliative effect, with a large amount of placebo effect, and a generous helping of time. What you get is an impressive recovery, regardless of what kind of treatment you receive. Whether you have your trigger points goaded, your acupoints punctured, your fixations mobilized, or your misalignments adjusted, you are likely to see some results. But, I advise you not to take any of it too seriously. Whatever method the Chiropractor uses is only based on speculation, and whatever relief it provides may only be temporary. Yet, it can be expensive, time-consuming and habit-forming — and — if it is done forcefully, there is always the possibility of harm from it. Rather than try to figure out all of the discrepancies and contradictions that exist within Chiropractic, 1 think it would be far better to just be free of it.

If you really want to do something constructive to achieve spinal health, I suggest that you study the Alexander Technique. It is not a therapy, rather it is an approach to movement awareness and movement education. The Alexander Technique involves learning how to move and use the body with poise and balance and ease and lightness. It requires the inhibition of habitual muscular tension and the projection of positive mental orders that serve to establish the correct relationship between the head, neck and back. The movements that flow from Alexander directions entail considerably less effort than habitual movements, and they are not associated with strain or pressure.

A person who is in pain needs to learn to inhibit maladaptive muscle tension and to restore, through conscious direction, a balanced resting state. Alexander training teaches you how to do this.

The Alexander Technique develops coordination. The pupil learns to allow the head to lead and the body to follow in each and every movement. A subtle lengthening of the spine takes place, as the pupil learns to "go up" in activity rather than "pull down". When the excessive and inappropriate muscle tension is eliminated, the body's anti-gravity reflexes can begin to operate without interference. The result is a fluid quality of movement that is free and expansive and completely unencumbered. There is no greater joy and pleasure in movement than that which can be attained with the Alexander Technique.

Alexander training will change the way you feel about exercise. How you move your body, qualitatively, will become more important than how far, or how fast, or how much you move it. With the Alexander Technique, the attainment of ease and lightness and smoothness in movement becomes the new objective.

Frederick Mathias Alexander was an Australian who lived from 1870 until 1955, and he was the father of body use education. He wrote four books, and the most highly acclaimed has always been **The Use of the Self**. There are several other excellent books on the Alexander Technique written by other authors. A very practical and easy one is **Back Trouble** by Deborah Caplan, who is both a physical therapist and an Alexander teacher. It is essentially an instructional manual on how to correctly use your neck and back in daily activities. The best theoretical and explanatory book is **The Alexander Technique** by Dr. Wilfred Barlow, who was Alexander's leading protégé. **Body Awareness in Action** by Professor Frank Pierce Jones offers an interesting historical perspective. Books on the Alexander Technique are available from Centerline Press, at 2005 Palo Verde, #325, Long Beach, CA 90815, phone:(213) 421-0220. Like many things in life, improved personal use can best be learned with the aid of a competent teacher. Fortunately, there Is a growing number of certified Alexander instructors in the United States, Canada, and elsewhere in the world. For a list of teachers in the United States you may contact The American Center for the Alexander Technique at either of the following locations:

129 West 67th Street, New York, NY 10023, (212) 799-0468

—or—

931 Elizabeth Street, San Francisco, CA 94114 (415) 282-8967

You may also contact the North American Society of Teachers of the Alexander Technique (NASTAT) at P.O. Box 3992, Champaign, IL 51826, (217) 359-3529,

Historically, there has been little connection between Natural Hygiene and the Alexander Technique, but I am hoping that this article will begin to change that. I would like to credit Dr. Alec Burton of Sydney, Australia for integrating both systems in his professional practice, and I would also like to thank him for introducing me to the Alexander Technique. I believe that training in the Alexander Technique should be seen as an integral part of Hygienic living. The two approaches are completely consistent in principle and entirely complementary in practice. In a straight line, they both lead you to health and freedom. In contrast, there is an army of therapists out there, of numerous persuasions, who are trying to steal your health freedom and subject you to a lifetime of dependency. I urge you to say "NO" and break free from therapeutic dependency as much as you possibly can.

Instead of spending money on Chiropractic, Acupuncture, or other such treatments, you could invest it in Alexander lessons. By so doing, you will obtain something of lasting value that you can use for the rest of your life. I have more to say about the Alexander Technique in the article that follows.

PERSONAL USE: THE ULTIMATE SELF-MASTERY

Personal use refers to the way in which you use your mind to direct and control your body. For most people, that means acting *habitually*. For example, when was the last time you thought about how to go about standing up from a seated position? Most people go their whole lives without ever giving it a conscious thought. If our habitual responses were always appropriate, there would be no problem. But, quite the contrary is true. Most people have significant defects in their muscular habits of which they are completely unaware.

We tend to think of the body as a mechanical device. With its complex system of ball and socket joints, hinges, levers and shock absorbers, it is easy to think of the body in purely mechanical terms. But a mere machine is not capable of autonomous neuromuscular response the way the body is. Anyone can lift up a box and place it on a table. It seems simple and straight-forward. But there are vast differences in the way this simple act can be perfomed.

In a purely mechanical sense, there are only a few considerations involved with movement, mainly force and weight and leverage. But, when physiology is brought to bear, we have to consider the balance and economy of muscle tension, the sequence of events, and the overall efficiency of the neuromuscular response.

Every action and movement involves the use of the entire body. You have to do something with every part of yourself whenever you do anything, even if it is just to allow that part to be still. A dentist works in tight spaces with his hands, and all of his attention is focused on what his hands are doing. But even though his mind is completely preoccupied with that, he is still doing something with his neck, with his back, with his shoulders, with his abdomen and with his breathing apparatus. He will be doing something with his hips and knees, often holding them tense and locked, when he should be keeping them free and balanced. The way most of us use ourselves is to focus completely upon our end (that is, our goal, our objective, our purpose), and to ignore completely our means (the series of steps that we employ to achieve our end). In performing both our daily activities and our specialized tasks, most of us never think about how we use ourselves. Perhaps when we lift something heavy, it occurs to us to keep our back straight, flex our knees and lift with our legs. This is mechanically sound, but it will not alone insure the smooth and efficient projection of neuromuscular energy, nor will it guard against excess strain and tension. Something more is needed.

Lifting is not the only time that we subject ourselves to strain. Most of us misuse ourselves when we walk, when we talk, when we sit, when we stand, when we eat and even when we attempt to rest. We never think about how we perform these activities; we do them in accordance with our habit. And for most of us, our habits, in relation to our personal use, are decidedly harmful.

Bad habits of posture and movement are probably the oldest and most deep-seated bad habits that people have. And they practice them, unknowingly, every moment of their waking lives, and perhaps even in their sleep. Excess muscle tension and faulty movement patterns not only can dissipate energy, they can disturb balance and equilibrium, both physically and psychologically. Chronic stress and uneasiness may begin on the psychological level, but it is quickly transferred into the muscular system. Learning to release the muscular manifestations of stress is just as important as making whatever psychological adjustments are necessary.

Practically everyone is familiar with stress reduction techniques, such as meditation, breathing exercises, relaxation procedures and self-hypnosis. Whether or not these methods are effective, they all suffer from one glaring deficiency: they are, what F.M. Alexander called "end-gaining procedures." They attempt to treat or remedy stress without dealing with the causes of stress and without dealing with the individual's total pattern of response. Stress is not caused by a lack of hypnosis or a failure to meditate or perform rituals. People do not need antidotes to stress. What they need is to learn how to respond to life's buffeting without stress.

Rather than submitting to the usual manual and electrical treatments, Hygienists should become students of the Alexander Technique. F. Mathias Alexander was an Australian actor and orator in the last decade of the 19th century. He developed a hoarse voice in performing and was sometimes unable to speak. He underwent numerous medical treatments to no avail. Then, it occurred to him that perhaps there was something wrong with the way he used himself that brought on the trouble. He set up mirrors to observe himself, and he discovered that whenever he attempted to speak, he would first thrust his head back, stiffen his neck, take a gasping breath and actually depress his larynx. These were deeply ingrained habits, but when he succeeded at inhibiting them, his voice problems disappeared. Alexander realized that his discovery had implications not just for speaking, but for all activities, and not just for himself, but for everyone. He spent years studying the physical and mental processes concerned with "the use of the self." He sailed to London in 1904 with the hope that his work would receive more attention there. He spent the rest of his life there, and in the United States, teaching, writing and training others to carry on his work. He died in London in 1955 at the age of 86.

Education in the Alexander technique consists of private lessons with a teacher who combines verbal orders with a delicate, physical handling (that is meant to be instructional, not therapeutic) to encourage a better head/neck relationship, improved muscular balance and a general lengthening of the body. The intent of the handling is not just to alter the positioning, but also the tensional balance. Perhaps Alexander's most important discovery was that the body has got to lengthen in activity. You have got to learn to "go up" rather than "pull down" when you move.

Alexander found out through patient experimentation that the problem lies in our sensory system, as well as in our motor system. The faulty ways in which we use ourselves feel right to us, because we have no other sensory standard with which to compare them. One of the objectives of the Alexander lesson is to give the student the "kinesthetic" experience, of moving with ease and lightness, perhaps for the first time in his memory.

Alexander commands are verbal orders that you give to yourself. The orders are given both sequentially and simultaneously, that is, you must continue to project the first order, as you go on to the second, and so on. But, it is very important that you just "think" the orders and not attempt to "do" them. If you react too quickly with a muscular response, you are bound to activate the tension patterns that already exist. In that event, nothing fundamentally different and better will happen. The way to bring about a fundamental change is to pause upon receiving a stimulus to act, inhibit your habitual response and allow the mental projection of the orders to bring about a new and better response. What I am describing is not a form of mysticism. It has been proven scientifically that thought can directly affect the electrical signals to muscles. Stroboscopic photography and electromyography were used at Tufts University by Professor Frank Pierce Jones to substantiate the physiological changes in muscle length and tension brought about by the Alexander Technique. I strongly urge you to read his book, *Body Awareness in Action.*

The following description of good body use is meant to introduce you to some important Alexander concepts, but keep in mind that it takes more than an intellectual understanding to master the Alexander Technique. There is no substitute for a good teacher.

In each and every movement, there should be a lengthening of the body, instead of a shortening. Most people lose several inches in height over the course of their adult lives. Gravity is blamed for it, but the truth is, that we bring it on ourselves. We pull down, instead of easing up, in movement. But, the capacity to go up depends upon the relationship between the head and the neck.

The head does not sit squarely on the neck. Most of the weight of the head is in front of the top joint. If the neck muscles release in back, it allows the head to move forward by virtue of its own weight. It is vitally important to allow the head to pivot forward because that is what takes the pressure off the neck. When the restraining action of the neck muscles in back is equal to, but not greater than, the force of the weight of the head going forward, then a genuine lengthening can take place. That perfect balance between the weight of the head in front and the tone of the neck muscles in back is what takes you up to your full height. The first Alexander order, therefore, is to: *"Allow the neck to be free, so that the head can go forward and up"*.

Alexander called the head/neck relationship the "primary control" because it sets the pattern for how you use your entire body. If you begin a movement by pulling your head back and stiffening and shortening your neck, it establishes a pattern of strain and tension that spreads to other regions. But, if you keep the head/neck joint free, and allow the neck muscles to lengthen, and direct the head forward and up, then you stand a good chance of moving your other joints freely as well.

The back then follows the upward movement of the head, as you give the order to: *"Allow the back to lengthen and widen"*. There should be only a slight arch in the properly used low back. Most of us make an artificial division of the back at the level of the waist, and it leads us to flex and extend the torso from the waist, instead of from the hips. Start thinking of your back as a functional unit that goes from your neck all the way down to your hips. The whole back has got to lengthen as it follows the upward movement of the head. But you must not lengthen at the expense of widening. Proper widening is what guarantees free and easy breathing. Your ribs have got to expand from below every time your breath comes in. Widening your back also provides more room for your internal organs, so that they function better and your abdomen does not protrude.

The next order is to: *"Allow the shoulders to release and widen"*. This allows the shoulder blades to flatten against the ribs and move laterally away from the spine. To allow lengthening in the muscles that suspend the shoulder blades is a difficult thing for most of us to do, but the effect is dramatic. Don't make the mistake of drawing your shoulders back or hunching them up. Just direct the shoulders outward. In standing, the arms will naturally tend to rotate internally so that the back of the hand faces more forward. You should be as broad as possible across your shoulders, both in front and in back.

In any kind of squatting action, the body should be allowed to pivot on its hinges, namely the knees and hips. The knees should never be locked, but should always be directed slightly forward, so as to avoid stiffening them. This not only protects your knees, but it also protects your low back. The ankles should be kept free, with more weight taken through the heels than through the front of the foot. This counterbalances the weight of the head, which, if you recall, is being directed forward and up.

This brief summary of Alexander directions gives you some idea of what it is about, but it does not really do it justice. The Alexander Technique is concerned primarily with how you use your body in the act of moving. The word "posture" does not suffice to describe its content, because posture is stationary, and Alexander work is not. Perhaps, we could speak of The Alexander Technique as "four dimensional posture," to include the process of movement, which takes place over time. But, Alexandrian inhibition of habitual muscular sets is essential in order to veto the old, dystonic patterns. Continually saying "NO" to inappropriate muscular habits is the centerpiece of the Alexander Technique.

The Alexander Technique attempts to impart conscious control through all phases of movement. It enables you to move your body smoothly and gracefully and with the greatest conservation of energy. In fact, using the Technique makes you feel ten pounds lighter because it takes less energy to move your body in accordance with Alexander principles. It puts gravity to work for you, instead of against you. No form of body work can compare with the Alexander Technique in value, and I encourage every health seeker to learn and practice it.

STRETCHING: ACTIVITY — OR — TREATMENT?

If you are one of those people who has always felt guilty about not doing enough stretching, perhaps you will be pleased to hear my point of view, that stretching is not necessarily good for you. I rarely do any deliberate stretching any more, for three main reasons: First, it is boring. Second, it is just as likely to cause injury as prevent it. And third, it is impossible to shorten one muscle without lengthening another, and therefore, natural activities provide all the stretching I need.

You may be thinking that it is perfectly natural to stretch. Don't animals stretch? Why shouldn't people?

Animals, like cats for instance, do their stretching instinctively, and I think it is fine for people to stretch that way, for example, in conjunction with yawning. But, there is a world of difference between the spontaneous stretch of a yawn and the arbitrary decision that, "Now it is time to touch my toes ten times." *That* you never see animals do. It is a contrived, artificial exercise, that can best be described as a tug-of-war with yourself. It could also be called self-administered therapy. (And my long-time readers know how I feel about that word.) Basically, in stretching, you are contracting one set of muscles to overcome the internal resistance of another set of muscles. In other words, you are applying force to yourself in a way that can be stressful and violent.

It is well known that muscles and ligaments have the inherent tendency to shorten. But, rather than being a destructive process, this is a protective mechanism. The function of your connective tissues is not only to allow and facilitate motion, but also to limit it. In fact, your connective tissues tighten up to the limit of motion of your regular activities. This provides the range of motion you need, while preserving the strength and passive resistance that protects you from injury. Flexibility is far from being an unqualified good. We need not emulate the yogis who can tie themselves into knots until they look like human pretzels. This is just another bizarre way of abusing the body.

If you learn to use your body in a free and open way, while allowing your back to lengthen and widen in activity, you will get all of the stretching you need in the course of living and breathing and moving. Stretching exercises really belong to the "remedy mentality." It is an attempt to use exercise as an antidote for misuse.

For years, I accepted the conventional wisdom that stretching was essential to keep my body flexible. I did my daily dozen faithfully, though I enjoyed it about as much as swallowing medicine. Finally, I quit, and to my pleasant surprise, I discovered that my spontaneous flexibility was entirely adequate to facilitate the activities of my life. What a relief it was, not to have to endure forced stretching procedures any longer. Now, I simply start slowly with my athletic endeavors, and only gradually work up to a vigorous pace. I have found that it is just as effective to warm up that way, as it is to stretch, and it is more likely to prevent injury. Granted, it may not be adequate preparation for such activities as the ballet and the martial arts; but, it is entirely adequate for the things I do, like walking and swimming and cycling. The point is, that you only need as much flexibility as your activities demand, and there is no great benefit in seeking more than that.

It is generally accepted that people become stiff and rigid as they age because they fail to do enough stretching, but that is not true. The stiffness is part and parcel of the way that people function in their daily lives, and it would be present in whatever stretching they did as well. The solution is not to resort to force (whether applied by oneself or by others), but rather, to learn how to release muscles into length, both when at rest and in activity. If we learn to consciously use the body correctly from moment to moment in our daily lives, we will have no need for stretching or any other "remedial" exercises.

A good time to cultivate improved personal use is when you are walking. As an exercise, walking is unique. There is a center in the brain that controls and facilitates the act of walking. It is the one activity you can most easily do without tightening up and shortening yourself and increasing the overall tension in your body.

In walking, your body can expand in all directions. There is an opening up and a freedom that you can increasingly gain as you walk. There is a perfect balance between muscular lengthening and muscular contraction in a walk, and therefore, walking requires no preliminary or compensatory stretching. It is truly the perfect exercise.

As you walk, think about keeping your neck muscles as free and lengthened as possible, and allow your head to lead the way, forward and up. Not by straining, but by giving positive mental directions, you should be as tall and as broad as you can be as you walk. Don't hold your chin up. You must inhibit that tendency if you have it. Allow your back to lengthen and widen, following the upward movement of your head. Release and widen your shoulders, so that your arms swing freely, but not because you forcibly swing them. Allow your hips to swivel freely, forward and back, but inhibit any side-to-side motion. Allow your knees to release forward over the top of each foot with every step.

Walk with a free and easy stride that does not entail reaching. Your legs want to travel a certain distance with each step. Your feet want to fall in a certain spot. Don't reach for more. If you wish to increase your speed, you can walk faster by moving your legs faster, but do not try to alter the length of your stride. However, you should not try to walk so fast that it interferes with the cadence of your walk or compromises your body's ability to expand.

Try to walk with a fairly narrow gait. When you come to rest, it is fine to separate your feet and take a broader stance. But, once you start to walk, there should be no more than several inches between the tracks of your feet. A wide gait converts a walk into a wobble.

If you walk smoothly and efficiently, your muscles will get both the stretching and the contracting they need, and all within the course of a perfectly natural activity.

As you walk, your body should be expanding in all directions. This expansion occurs through your head upwards. It occurs through your shoulders out to the sides. It occurs through your knees forward with each step. It occurs through your ribs and back laterally with each breath. You are getting taller, broader, and taking up more space in the universe with every step you take.

If you insist on stretching, you should learn to do it correctly. The way to do so would be to move to the limit of the functional range that has already been established by your everyday activities, and then go just a little bit further to increase it. It takes a great deal of sensitivity and control to do this without straining. And perhaps it is most important to remember that you must never compromise the total pattern of use of your whole body for the sake of the partial pattern that may be involved with the stretch. The increased range that comes from a stretching procedure will only be maintained if it is repeated often. If you do not intend to practice your stretching exercises daily, it would probably be better not to do them at all. Instead, just learn how to use yourself well within the natural range of motion that springs from your ordinary activities. There is no absolute amount of flexibility that you must have in order to be healthy and to function well.

Of course, some people really enjoy their stretching exercises, and I am sure that the advocates of stretching will have plenty to say in opposition to my point of view. But, no matter how many specific situations you can name where you think stretching is indispensable, I ask that you at least recognize that the human body was meant to function naturally and spontaneously in useful and practical activities without the need for remedial measures.

INSTINCT
— VERSUS —
REASON

There is only one fundamental alternative in the universe: existence or non-existence — and it pertains to a single class of entities: to living organisms. The existence of inanimate matter is unconditional, the existence of life is not: it depends on a specific course of action. Matter is indestructible; it changes its forms, but it cannot cease to exist. It is only a living organism that faces a constant alternative: the issue of life or death. Life is a process of self-sustaining and self-generated action. If an organism fails in that action, it dies; its chemical elements remain, but its life goes out of existence. It is only the concept of "Life" that makes the concept of "Value" possible. It is only to a living entity that things can be good or evil.

Man has no automatic code of survival. His particular distinction from all other living species is his necessity to act in the face of alternatives by means of volitional choice. He has no automatic knowledge of what is good for him or evil, what values his life depends on, what course of action it requires. Are you prattling about an instinct of self-preservation? An instinct is an unerring and automatic form of knowledge. A desire is not an instinct. A desire to live does not give you the

knowledge required for living. Man must obtain his knowledge and choose his actions by a process of thinking, which nature will not force him to perform. Man has the power to act as his own destroyer - and that is the way he has acted throughout most of history.

—Ayn Rand
from **Atlas Shrugged**

It has been said that "instinctive living" is the essence of Natural Hygiene. Accordingly, as Hygienists, we should get in touch with our instincts, and always follow what they dictate. By this philosophy, instincts are infallible, and they cannot possibly lead us astray. Instinctual guidance, therefore, is all we ever need to live healthfully.

I see this as a dangerous philosophy. Instincts, like the desire to eat when you are hungry, drink when you are thirsty, and sleep when you are tired, do point us in the right direction. But, are they always sufficient to guide human behavior? The answer clearly is "No." All you can say is that *generally* instincts are reliable. But, there certainly are times when instinctual guidance is inadequate.

Consider first the matter of over-eating. Does instinct prevent us from over-eating? Imagine that it is a beautiful summer's day, and you are in the orchard picking cherries. The cherries are sweet and plump and crisp and tangy, and each one explodes in your mouth with a burst of flavor and juiciness. How many could you eat before your body says, "No more!"? If you are anything like me, I imagine it is quite a lot, perhaps more than would be good for you. You might have to tell yourself, "That's enough," even though you feel like you could eat more. It would be reason talking to you - not instinct. Instinct would eventually signal you to stop by making you feel "full," but by then, you would have already over-eaten. Instinct sometimes does not "kick-in" soon enough to prevent us from over-eating. If you want proof, look at animals. They live entirely by instinct, and they are certainly capable of over-eating. When given something that is unusually tasty, horses are known to eat until they are severely bloated and ill. Breeders keep a close eye on the amount of food given to their prize steeds. Laboratory rats, when allowed to feed "ad libitum," eat until they become fat and sassy, and they tend to die young of degenerative diseases. You really cannot rely on instinct to prevent you from over-eating. You have to consciously decide not to do it.

Next, let's look at exercise. Imagine that it is the first warm day of Spring. You've been trapped indoors all winter, and now you are out in the fresh air and sunshine, running through the park, enjoying the green grass, the sparkling sun, and the blue sky. It feels wonderful to be moving along on your own power. You feel like a deer prancing through the woods. But, this is your first run of the season, and you know that you could very easily pull a muscle or strain a tendon if you overdo it. So, you don't wait until you feel sore before you stop. You play it safe and quit well ahead of time, even though you feel like running more. In that case, you would not be acting on instinct; you would be acting on reason.

Thirst is a sensitive and finely-tuned mechanism for controlling water intake, and most of the time, it is perfectly reliable. But, there are exceptions. Endurance athletes, who race and train for long periods in the heat, know that they have to drink frequently in order to avoid dehydration. Yet, the exercise tends to be distracting. If they wait for thirst to appear, it is likely that they will have already incurred a water deficit. It is much better, under these extreme conditions, to err on the side of caution and drink ahead of time. This preventive action is derived from knowledge and experience - not from instinct.

Sunshine is wonderful, unless you get too much of it. But, how do you know when you've had too much? If you wait until you feel hot and sore and irritated to seek shelter, your skin will have already been damaged. You have to intelligently seek cover ahead of time. If you wait upon instinct, you just might get burned.

My last example requires no elaboration. Who in his right mind would suggest that instinct is a reliable guide to action concerning sex? What does instinct know about unwanted pregnancies? What does instinct know about venereal diseases? What does instinct know about broken homes and families? If there is one area where reason should definitely be in the driver's seat, it is the area of sex.

Although our instincts may be "pure" in the beginning, over time they tend to become jumbled with our feelings, desires, cravings, impulses and whims. Sometimes, we think that we are responding instinctively, when we are really responding to habit, or even to irritation. We think that we are hungry, when really we are tired. We think that we are thirsty, when really we are suffering with gastric distress. We think that we are energized when really we are just stimulated. Can we always know that what we are experiencing is a true and noble instinct, and not something else? It is not always easy to tell.

In conclusion, instincts are wholesome and good, but they are not adequate by themselves to guide human behavior. Hygiene is not the practice of instinctive living. Hygiene is the practice of intelligent living. You should always pay attention to what your instincts are telling you, but let reason decide whether or not to act on them. In the final analysis, you do what you determine to be in your best interest, whether or not it is in keeping with your instincts. Granted, that most of the time, reason and instinct are in accord, especially for someone living Hygienically. But, as I have shown, there can be exceptions. When a conflict does arise between reason and instinct, let reason decide.

THE LAW OF UNIFORM EFFECT

The renowned *New England Journal of Medicine* made front page news in May of 1986 with the startling announcement that two independent research studies had found a significant link between alcohol consumption and the incidence of breast cancer in women. It was found that even one drink per day could increase the risk of developing breast cancer by 60 to 100%.

This news was hardly startling to Hygienists because we have long regarded alcohol as a protoplasmic poison.

But, what is significant, is that the same *New England Journal of Medicine* has reported on other occasions that moderate alcohol consumption actually protects against heart disease. We are supposed to believe that one substance, ethyl alcohol, promotes coronary health at the same time that it causes mammary disease. Alcohol, by this way of thinking, is a friend to the heart and a foe to the breast. How it affects the other organs of the body is anybody's guess. We won't know until the research comes in. In the end, there will be two columns: "FOR" and "AGAINST." And every organ and body part will be assigned to one category or the other, depending upon how it is affected by alcohol. Then, each of us can decide whether or not to drink, depending upon which organs we value most.

All joking aside, this medical model is completely untenable. Regardless of what the researchers think, the human body is not a collection of independent organs, each living its own life, and each relating in its own way to the environment. Breast cells and heart cells develop from the same fertilized ovum. They contain the exact, same genetic blueprint. They perform the same basic cellular functions, pertaining to nutrition and drainage, as well as their own specialized functions. Their requirements for survival are the same. Their biological needs are the same. The laws of life pertain to breast cells in the exact same manner as they pertain to heart cells. What nourishes breast cells, nourishes heart cells. What poisons breast cells, poisons heart cells. The difference between the two lies in the fact that they are found in different locations and that they perform different functions, not that they live in different realities.

The only correct way of viewing the human body is to view it as a whole. At the beginning of life, all parts of the body are one, and though differentiation takes place, there is still always continuity. Differentiation occurs as a means of increasing efficiency and productiveness. Specialized cells acquire specialized structural and functional characteristics, but they are still alike, being made of the same, protoplasmic "stuff" and being dependent upon the same, supportive materials and influences. The different cells of the body have essentially the same needs, and the different organs of the body act in complete accord in how they relate to elements from the outside. What I am getting at, is that there is no way that alcohol could be good for the heart and bad for the breast. It would break a law of Nature for that to be true (and her laws are inviolable). So, let's take a closer look at the evidence.

The most publicized study that linked alcohol with protection against heart disease was done by Dr. Arthur Klatsky, a cardiologist at Kaiser Permanente Medical Center, in Oakland, California, in 1978. He found that non-drinkers were more apt to be hospitalized for coronary heart disease than people who had one or two drinks per day. Even patients who took three or more drinks per day were less likely to be hospitalized for coronary heart disease than non-drinkers.

The first thing that occurs to me in reviewing this study is that there are numerous reasons why a person with coronary heart disease might not be hospitalized. Not every sick person has medical insurance or the means to pay for hospitalization. Not every heart disease victim lives long enough to be hospitalized. Many of them die suddenly of vascular accidents without a previous medical history of the disease. Moreover, there are a lot of people who just don't like going to the hospital. They'd rather stay home.

Among the non-drinkers, there could be a large number of ex-drinkers, who quit drinking after they developed coronary heart disease. In our society, people generally have a reason for being "teetotalers," and often that reason is ill-health. In fact, a man could drink alcohol for six or seven decades and suffer the consequences of it, but on the day he quits, he would instantly become a non-drinker and be counted as such.

Perhaps my speculations are no better than theirs, but why from this meager statistic concerning hospital admissions, make a flying, intellectual leap and conclude that alcohol protects the heart? Is it because they were trying to prove that from the start? It brings to mind the famous words of Mark Twain, that - "There are lies, damn lies and statistics."

Even Dr. Klatsky acknowledged that alcohol can cause cardiomyopathy, a fatal degeneration of the heart muscle. This was the affliction that troubled Barney Clark, the man who received the first artificial heart. Does it seem possible that alcohol could damage the heart muscle, yet protect the adjacent blood vessels that course through it, which are also composed of muscle? Does it not seem like a safer and more prudent bet to assume that alcohol is deleterious to every cell and tissue of the human body, without exception?

In Natural Hygiene, we believe that life is orderly, not chaotic. We believe in the Law of Cause and Effect. We know that contradictions can never exist in reality, but only in our perceptions.

So, when faced with what appears to be a contradiction, we know that we must go back and check our premises and look for an error. Invariably, one will be found.

The truth is that there are no saving graces to alcohol. It is a poison, pure and simple. It is poisonous in large amounts, and it is poisonous in small amounts. It is poisonous in youth, and it is poisonous in old age. It is poisonous in health, and it is poisonous in disease. It is poisonous to every square inch of the human body. Every sip of alcohol taken is an act of self-destruction.

The Law of Uniform Effect states this principle succinctly:

The influence of any substance upon the various organs of the body is always in the same direction, as being either favorable or unfavorable, usable or non-usable, life-supporting or life-threatening. Each and every cell relates in essentially the same way to either appropriate or reject the substance. It is impossible for a substance to be a boon to one organ and a bane to another.

WHERE THE JOURNEY LEADS

The truth should be self-evident that any method or system that destroys the independence and autonomy of the individual and makes him forever dependent upon another man, or class of men, is not natural. Any system that of itself creates a privileged class who can, by law, or otherwise, lord over their fellow men, destroys true freedom and personal autonomy. Any system that teaches the sick that they can get well only through the exercise of the skill of someone else, or through the operation of something else, and that they remain alive only through the tender mercies of the privileged class, has no place in Nature's scheme of things, and the sooner it is abolished, the better will Mankind be. It was no more a part of the original scheme of things that Man should be supplicate at the feet of healers than that lions or cod-fish should be. It cannot be that Mankind will forever be dependent upon the tender mercies of the doctor and his bag of tricks. It matters not whether Man is dependent on the physician for his drugs, on the Chiropractor to adjust his spinal column, on the psychoanalyst for mental catharsis, or on the miracle monger as a medium through which to receive mystic emanations; he is a slave to that class upon which he depends. *Therapeutics makes slaves of men.* This is an evil and it cannot endure.

— *Dr. Herbert M. Shelton*
from Human Life: Its Philosophy and Laws.

There may have been a time in the distant past when living a healthful life occurred automatically. But, to live Hygienically today, you have got to do it by conscious choice. To avoid destructive habits and influences is something you must deliberately choose, or otherwise, they are likely to be thrust upon you.

But, why should you live Hygienically? You are not going to live forever, no matter what you do. Furthermore, whether you live to 85 or 90 or some other advanced age, it is just a number, and it really doesn't matter. What matters is that your life be good right *now*. What matters is that you have a good day, *today*. Each and every day you practice it, Hygienic living should increase your capacity to enjoy life and be happy. And nowhere is this more true than in connection with the simple pleasures in life.

Your capacity to enjoy a beautiful sight, a glorious sound, a warm touch or an inspiring effort is enhanced by the rise in your perceptive powers that results from Hygienic living. And this is the most important thing that Hygiene can do for you: to make you more available for the things in life that really give you joy and satisfaction and fulfillment. Hygiene should free you up so that you can live your life more fully and abundantly.

Imagine that it is morning. You have just awakened, and the first thing you do is swallow down a handful of vitamin pills and capsules. It isn't easy to do, even with a big gulp of water. They seem to get stuck in your throat and they hit your stomach with a plop. There is an unpleasant smell and aftertaste that make you *shudder* briefly. At least you got it over with, until it is time for the next dose. Now imagine that you are 87-years old. It is morning again, and you perform the exact same ritual of taking your vitamins that you have been performing every morning for all the intervening years and decades. It is no more pleasant now than it was in the beginning. It is even more difficult for you to swallow all the pills. You look back on all the years of pill-popping and wonder if it was worthwhile.

Now return to the present. It is morning again. This time, instead of reaching for vitamins, you enter the kitchen, and there is a giant, striped watermelon sitting on the counter. It has that slightly golden hue on one side telling you that it is perfectly ripe. You cut into it, and it literally snaps open. You sit down to eat a slice, and you think that it is the sweetest and most refreshing melon you have ever eaten. Now imagine again that you are 87, and that you're again eating melon for breakfast, as you have done every morning for all of the intervening years and decades. You think back on all those delightful melons. Could there possibly be any regrets? Could there be any possible doubts about the rightness of what you've done?

Every aspect of Hygiene is like that. Every Hygienic practice leaves you feeling good about yourself and your behavior. Every Hygienic practice is satisfying and fulfilling, not just in the result it brings, but in the very act of doing it.

Sickness is a nuisance. Going in for treatment is an inconvenience (and often a torture). Having to worry about yourself is a distraction and a drain. Hygiene can strip away these burdens (that are such a big part of most people's lives) and leave you more time for the things you really enjoy doing. So, make that the standard by which you judge the attractiveness of any health option. Before you decide to go in for colonic irrigations or chelation treatments or herbal implants, ask yourself if it is something that will lead you to greater health and freedom and personal autonomy? Could you see yourself doing it on a regular basis for the rest of your life and enjoying it? Does it give you less to worry about and hassle with and pay for, or more?

Of course, there are times when therapeutic intervention is the only way to solve a health problem. A cataract is not going to go away without surgery. Neither will a massive, prostatic obstruction. A dental abscess must be drained and filled. A fracture has got to be set and immobilized. I am not opposed to treatment when it is necessary. But I am opposed to the idea of people weaving therapy into their lives on a permanent basis if they don't have to. Therapy, in that instance, becomes a limiting and complicating factor in their lives (and often a harmful one). Such treatment may seem like a blessing at first, but it winds up becoming an unmitigated burden. I am speaking of symptomatic medicine, whether it is modern or ancient, Eastern or Western, allopathic or homeopathic. I am speaking of physical medicine, whether it is chiropractic, osteopathic, acupuncture, rolfing or whatever. These things are all therapeutic traps. It is so easy to get hooked on them.

Even massage is something that people should be careful about. I am not opposed to people touching each other. But, I see it as a personal need rather than a therapeutic one. When a mother strokes her child, it is an expression of love and tenderness; there is no reason to equate it with therapy. I think it is fine if people undergo massage as a pleasant and enjoyable experience. Massage feels good; it is relaxing and comforting. But the minute you get serious about it, and start using massage as a frequent remedy, and start seeking increasingly intense and aggressive methods, then it becomes just as addictive as any other therapy. *Force* is just not the answer in the vast majority of cases. The answer, most often, is *to correct the manner of use*. How is the person eating and drinking? How is the person moving and working and playing? How is the person supporting his weight and maintaining his balance? How is the person thinking and responding? How is the person reacting to stressful events? How is the person resting and conserving? Correct the manner of use, and everything else falls into place. That is why I have said repeatedly that Natural Hygiene, in combination with the Alexander Technique, is truly the best way to grow towards health and freedom.

What I ask of the reader is not to always and automatically reject therapy, but just not to worship it. Don't accept the rationales of therapists without some healthy skepticism. Don't give therapy the benefit of the doubt as being attractive and desirable. Realize that long-term therapy is often more of a burden than a solution.

Consider that a therapist is someone who has adopted a particular diagnostic and therapeutic *bias* that he is trying to pass on to you. If he is an allergist, he will probably discover a host of things to which you are allergic, and for which you need specific injections. If he is a chiropractor, he is sure to find subluxations in your spine requiring numerous adjustments. If she practices "environmental medicine," she will probably link your problems to molds and Candida, calling for anti-yeast medications. If she is a nutritionist, you can bet that numerous vitamin and mineral "deficiencies" are going to be uncovered requiring extensive supplementation. If you go to a psychiatrist, expect to be told that you have a "chemical imbalance" in your brain calling for "psychotropic" drugs.

The point is that a practitioner tends to become oriented in a certain therapeutic direction, and tends to find things wrong with people in a way that justifies the specific treatment regimen he or she employs. The explanation given by a therapist usually sounds plausible. But, there are undoubtedly other explanations that would be given by other therapists in the same situation that would sound equally plausible. If you step back and look at the whole picture, you begin to see that there is a bonafide therapeutic circus going on out there.

I should think that people would get tired of bouncing around from one therapist to the next. If you look past therapeutic babble in all its forms, you realize that the only thing that is absolutely real for you is your life and how you live it. And that is the beauty of Hygiene; it deals only with things that are absolutely and positively real. You *have to eat,* so why not try to obtain the best food you can? You *have to breathe,* so why not try to locate yourself where the air is clean? You *have to move,* so why not engage in activities that bring joy to motion? There is no question that these things are good. Their value is not derived from sophisticated theories or complicated tests, or elaborate sales pitches, but rather from the primordial requisites of human life. Is it so far-fetched to think that living a biologically normal life is the most certain way to achieve health and happiness?

Remember that there are people in the world who never have anything done to them *therapeutically* who are doing just fine. I am one of them. My health? It's good. My back? It's strong. My energy? It's high. I feel good within my body, and no one lays a hand on me therapeutically. While others are hanging around the offices of chiropractors, acupuncturists and other therapists, I am out on my bicycle, touring the beautiful Texas countryside. While some people are taking coffee enemas and herbal implants as a health ritual, I am playing the piano. While others are spending hard-earned money on nauseating vitamins and antioxidants, I am feasting on mangos. And realize that I say these things only because I want as much for you as I have for myself. I am not Superman. Anything that I can do, others can do. With a modest income, I enjoy a high quality of life, which I owe to Natural Hygiene, and I want nothing less for you.

I AM FREE! And I want you to be free.

ORGANIZATIONS

I urge you to contact the following excellent organizations about becoming a member, or for more information on the Natural Hygiene health maintenance system:

The American Natural Hygiene Society
P.O. Box 30630
Tampa, Florida 33630
Contact Person: James Lennon   Phone (813) 855-6607

The Canadian Natural Hygiene Society
P.O. Box 235, Station "T"
Toronto, Ontario
Canada M6B 4A1
Contact Persons: Gladys Aaron   Phone: (416) 781-0359

GetWell ★ StayWell, America!
1776 ★ The Hygiene Joy Way!
Mount Vernon, Washington 98273
Contact Person: Victoria BidWell   Phone: (206) 428 - 3687

Natural Hygiene, Inc.
P.O. Box 2132, Huntington Station
Shelton, Connecticut 06484
Contact Person: Jo Willard   Phone: (203) 929 - 1557

SUGGESTED READING

For a full presentation of the health maintenance system known as Natural Hygiene, I recommend any of these books .

The Myth of Neurosis by Garth Wood, M.D.

How I Found Freedom in an Unfree World, by Harry Browne

The Psychology of Self-Esteem, by Nathaniel Brandon

Food For Life, by Neal Barnard, M.D.

The Power of Your Plate, by Neal Barnard, M.D..

Follies and Fallacies in Medicine, by Skrabanek & McCormick

Medical Drugs on Trial? Verdict Guilty!, by Keki Sidhwa D.O.

Superior Nutrition, by Herbert Shelton

The Science and Fine Art of Fasting, by Herbert Shelton

Fasting Can Save Your Life, by Herbert Shelton

The McDougall Plan, by John McDougall, M.D.

McDougall's Medicine, by John McDougall, M.D.

Diet for a New America, by John Robbins

The Health Seeker's Yearbook, by Victoria Bidwell

Vegan Nutrition: Pure and Simple, by Michael Klaper, M.D.

The Recovery of Culture, by Henry Bailey Stevens

The Alexander Technique, by Wilfred Barlow, M.D.

Medical Nemesis, by Ivan Illich

Food Reform: Our Desperate Need, by Robin Hur

Sunlight, by Zane Kime, M.D.

The Use of Self, by Frederick, M. Alexander

Back Trouble, by Deborah Caplan

Other Health-Related Materials from MONARCH

NATURALLY HIGH
INTERNALLY WELL
Reclaiming and Owning the Power to Heal Yourself
Dr. Howard Levine

This book of alternative health care options will pave the way for many people to achieve a stronger and healthier body. **Naturally High, Internally Well** explains Dr. Howard Levine's personal philosophy toward the natural health care field.

His extensive practical experience and research provide those people seeking alternatives to standard medicine a starting point to developing new health and wellness.

The book deals extensively with issues such as the philosophy of empowerment, whereby decisions to make adjustments in lifestyle are firmly based on factual information rather than myth or lore, developing nutritional flexibility, and provides a list for comparison of a number of Complementary Health Care options, together with some of their approaches and ideals.

ISBN 1-895952-00-X   **$12.95**

KICKING YOUR STRESS HABITS
A Do-it yourself Guide for Coping with Stress
Donald A. Tubesing

} ... helps you get to the roots of your stress reactions and modify them. ~
— The New York Times

Over a quarter of a million people have discovered how **Kicking Your Stress Habits** can work for them — and it can work for you!

The book contains down-to-earth examples, challenging worksheets, creative coping alternatives and step-by-step action planning guides, to provide individuals or groups with a complete resource for stress management, and a valuable learning tool.

ISBN 0-938586-009   **$19.95**

• •

SEEKING YOUR HEALTHY BALANCE
A Do-it-yourself Guide to Whole Person Well-being
Donald A. Tubesing and
Nancy Loving Tubesing

How do you successfully juggle all of your daily responsibilities and still remain healthy?

Seeking Your Healthy Balance gives you insight into juggling work, self, and others; clarifying self-care options; and discovering personal priorities.

ISBN 0-938586-459   **$19.95**

SENSATIONAL RELAXATION

When stress piles up, it becomes a heavy load to bear - a physical and emotional burden.

Experience the liberating power of stress relief with these full-length relaxation experiences. Each appeals to the senses and teaches specific relaxation techniques and skills that can be used again and again.

Each cassette: $12.95

Countdown to Relaxation	**ISBN 0-938586-82-3**
Daybreak/Sundown	**ISBN 0-938586-83-1**
Take a Deep Breath	**ISBN 0-938586-93-9**
Relax... Let Go... Relax	**ISBN 0-938586-94-7**
Stress Release	**ISBN 0-938586-92-0**
Warm and Heavy	**ISBN 1-57025-000-6**

STRESSBREAKS

Relaxation for Stress Management

StressBreaks are short and sweet, designed to be used as an energy booster or a short time-out from stress. Try one of these healthy pick-me-ups or tension relievers whenever you need a change of pace.

Each Cassette: $12.95

Break Time	**ISBN 0-938586-84-X**
Natural Tranquilizers	**ISBN 0-938586-85-8**

GUIDED MEDITATION

Beyond relaxation lies the connection between body and mind. Wellness-oriented meditation unites the physical self with inner wisdom for growth, healing, and positive life change. Full-length guided meditations and imagery help listeners connect their inner values, meanings, and spiritual strengths. Use the meditations over and over again as a guide and a catalyst for

insight, centering, and balancing - or to deal with chronic pain.

Each Cassette: $12.95

Inner Healing	**ISBN 0-938586-80-7**
Personal Empowering	**ISBN 0-938586-81-5**
Healthy Balancing	**ISBN 1-57025-001-4**
Spiritual Centering	**ISBN 1-57025-002-2**

WILDERNESS DAYDREAMS

For those who find comfort, relaxation, and healing in nature - eight special journeys into the wilderness. Guided imagery evokes the sensations of tranquil natural settings: a campfire... a marsh meadow... a placid lake... and many more.

Each Cassette: $12.95

Wilderness Daydreams 1:	**ISBN 1-57025-003-0**
Wilderness Daydreams 2:	**ISBN 1-57025-004-9**
Wilderness Daydreams 3:	**ISBN 1-57025-005-7**
Wilderness Daydreams 4:	**ISBN 0-938586-86-6**

DAYDREAMS

Imaging is an easy, natural process you use hundreds of times a day - any time you visualize the face of a loved one, mentally hum a favourite tune, recall or anticipate the taste of a special food. This same valuable process can help you relax when you're in a tough spot or after a busy day, by visualizing peaceful, comforting images.

Each Cassette: $12.95

Daydreams 1: Get-Aways   ISBN 0-938586-78-5

Daydreams 2: Peaceful Places   ISBN 0-938586-79-3

● ●

ORDER FORM

Please send your order including cheque, money order, VISA, or Mastercard number to:

MONARCH BOOKS OF CANADA
5000 Dufferin Street,
Downsview, Ontario, M3H 5T5
(800) 404-7404, FAX: (416) 736-1702

SHIPPING/HANDLING CHARGES: $4.00 ON ORDERS UP TO $75.00, AND 6% OF NET ORDER OVER $75.00. PLEASE ALLOW 4 - 6 WEEKS FOR DELIVERY

Payment Enclosed: ___ VISA, ___ Mastercard,

___ Cheque, ___ Money Order (Payable to "Monarch Books")

Card Number: _____

Expiry Date: _____

Name: _____

Address: _____

_____

Province/State: _____ Postal Code/Zip: _____

Telephone #: (____)_____